NO WORRY CURRIES

ALI & MUNSIF ABBASI'S
NO WORRY
CURRIES
Authentic Indian Home Cooking

ANGELS' SHARE®

The Angels' Share is an imprint of
Neil Wilson Publishing Ltd
303a The Pentagon Centre
36 Washington Street
GLASGOW
G3 8AZ

Tel: 0141 221 1117
Fax: 0141 221 5363
E-mail: info@nwp.sol.co.uk
www.nwp.co.uk
www.angelshare.co.uk

A catalogue record for this book is available
from the British Library.

ISBN 1-903238-51-X
Designed by Belstane
Printed in Finland by WS Bookwell

CONTENTS

FOREWORD

Having a curry is much more than simply satisfying hunger pangs – it means sitting down with friends, switching off from the usual pressures and getting stuck into some of the best food around.

As Ali and Munsif Abbasi know, and my waistline testifies, I enjoy a curry far too often. My tastes are fairly simple, as Ali and Munsif will remember having cooked a number of curries for my family over the last few years. They have tried to tempt me to broaden my tastes with more exotic spices and interesting recipes and I applaud them for their perseverance. However, I remain firmly fond of the simple chicken tikka balti – after a few tasty starters, of course.

My family, thankfully, are a little more adventurous and have thoroughly enjoyed all of the Abbasis' culinary experiments. I am sure that anyone buying this book will also discover that there's more to Ali Abbasi than keeping us on the right road and having us doubled up with laughter. He can also come up with a range of recipes to tempt every curry lover across the country while making sure that charities benefit too.

I am delighted to recommend this book and wish all of you many happy hours in the kitchen.

JACK MCCONNELL
FIRST MINISTER OF SCOTLAND

INTRODUCTION

Indian food has evolved into one of the most popular cuisines in the UK, and especially Scotland. In fact, chicken tikka masala is now said to be the UK's national dish.

In putting this book of recipes together we have sought to reveal the traditional and simple methods of cooking. This is entirely different to what is served in restaurants. We are sure you'll be surprised at the varied tastes on offer in this book and how simple it is to achieve them.

Many of our friends say curry is popular because it is what every late-night drinker craves after a few too many lagers. Eating a curry is always an enjoyable experience, whenever it is eaten, and the British have a love affair with spices and herbs that goes back centuries.

For a long time, many Indian curry restaurants outside the big cities got away with providing sub-standard meals at ridiculous prices. These days, however, you can get a great curry wherever you are in Scotland, be it Bonar Bridge, Kirkwall, Tobermory, Stornoway, Buckie or Galashiels.

We have often been asked what the difference is between a restaurant curry and a home-made curry. The main difference is obviously the length of time available for cooking and preparation. Restaurants have a wide range of dishes on offer and they prepare a basic curry sauce that they adapt in order to create different tasting curries. In general, if you take two fairly popular dishes, for example, chicken bhuna and chicken korma, the difference is a couple of minutes in the preparation process: the same sauce from the same sauce pot with the same cooked chicken. The secret is two frying pans – one with cream and coconut and the other with peppers and tomatoes. They are both ready in five minutes.

Home-made Indian cooking does not require the same urgency or preparation – the ingredients are allowed to cook and marry with the sauce in one pot to create a more authentic Indian taste. Many of the dishes might appear to have similar ingredients but the amount of each ingredient and when it is added helps to create the individual dish.

Both of us have had experience in Indian restaurants, in the kitchen and front-of-house. The experience gained was very useful but the cuisine was not always great. Any Asian will tell you that home cooking is superior to the restaurant fare. The training given to a worker in a restaurant prepares them for fast production and quick service. In any Indian restaurant you'll find there's a separate pot cooking the meal for the staff at the end of the night ... the good stuff, the stuff that has been given the correct time to cook and made in the traditional home-style. Some restaurants even offer the 'staff curry' on the menu. Try it if you get the chance.

The quality of Indian food in restaurants varies dramatically, but don't get us wrong, generally the standard of food in Indian restaurants is good. And don't let anyone tell you that there are secret ingredients in Indian cooking, there aren't. Just practice the recipes in this book and take a visit to your local Asian food store. Eventually you will be able to tell what ingredients are in a dish, and with experience you'll be able to judge the amount of each ingredient and the techniques you need. This book concentrates on flavour and technique and allows you to take the necessary time to go through the cooking procedure.

Don't rush things, and above all don't panic. We hope you'll work your way through all the recipes in this book and enjoy what you make. And remember: no worries!

ALI AND MUNSIF ABBASI

PS: Ali would also like to thank Angus MacDonald and family from the Braes on the Isle of Skye for providing the perfect peace and quiet in the shadow of the Cuillins while compiling these recipes.

1. KITCHEN ESSENTIALS

There is nothing worse than starting to prepare an Indian dish only to find that three-quarters of the way through the recipe you go to get some chillies and you find you have none. These are essential spices and ingredients that you should try to keep in your cupboard. Some are fresh, some are dried.

AJWAIN
Closely related to cumin and used in many dishes. Similar to thyme in flavour.

CARDAMOM
These pods have a slightly pungent but very aromatic taste and come in three varieties: green, white or black. They are used to flavour many curry dishes.

CHILLIES
Available fresh (red or green) or as powder or as ground, dried chillies (usually red). You can also buy whole pickled chillies.

Green chillies are the mildest form and red chillies are the hottest, these are dried in the sun and ground to a fine, fiery powder.

CINNAMON
One of the earliest-known spices. Cinnamon can be bought and used as bark sticks or powder.

CLOVES
These are used to flavour many curry dishes and are nearly always used whole. (Also good for toothache.)

CORIANDER
This comes in three forms: seed, powder and leaves. The seed is used when the dish is needed to be more aromatic. The lacy, green leaves are used as a fragrant garnish. The powder gives more flavour to a curry sauce.

FENNEL

These tiny seeds lend a delicate aniseed flavour to curry dishes. They are particularly good with vegetable dishes.

FENUGREEK

Used in leaf form, these are used to flavour both meat and vegetable dishes and are particularly useful in removing the 'fishiness' from seafood.

GARAM MASALA

This is a mixture of ground spices, including cloves, cardamoms, cumin and coriander.

GARLIC

This is absolutely essential in cooking Indian curries. For freshness choose only firm bulbs. Some garlic can be kept in its 'lazy' form – already chopped and preserved in a light vinegar, but the taste is not the same – so go for fresh if you can and keep 'lazy' garlic for emergencies.

The recipes in this book often call for the use of garlic pulp. For this, take about five garlic bulbs, and soak in water overnight, making them easier to peel. The next day peel and grind them in a food processor, adding a little water to make a pulp. The pulp can be stored in airtight containers in the fridge for 3-4 weeks. Alternatively, pour the individual pulps in ice cube trays and freeze. Use as and when required.

MANGO POWDER

This sour-tasting mango powder is made from dried raw mangoes.

ONION SEEDS

Black in colour and triangular in shape, these little seeds are used for both pickles and curries.

ROOT GINGER

This can be bought as preserved, fresh root or ground spice. It is an important ingredient in many curries and should always be peeled before use. You can also freeze fresh root ginger and it can be peeled easily while still frozen. It thaws quickly so there is no excuse to run out.

The recipes in this book often call for the use of ginger pulp. For this, take a large piece of root, and soak in water overnight making it easier to peel. The next day peel and grind in a food processor, adding a little water to make a pulp. The pulp can be stored in airtight containers in the fridge for 3-4 weeks. Alternatively, pour the individual pulps in ice cube trays and freeze, and use as and when required.

SAFFRON
This is the world's most expensive spice and has a unique flavour and fragrance. Fortunately, only a small quantity is needed to flavour or a colour a dish.

SESAME
Sesame is one of the most important oil seeds in the world. The sesame seed is a pale creamy colour.

SOY SAUCE
Made from a mixture of fermented soya beans, flour and water.

TAMARIND (Imli)
The dried pods of the tamarind, also known as the Indian date. Tamarind is sour and sticky and is added to a range of Indian dishes to add a distinctive tangy taste. Tamarind paste can be bought in jars.

TURMERIC
This is the ground root of a plant grown mostly in India. It is used mainly for colour (golden yellow) as it imparts little flavour.

Nine times out of ten, you will be able to get all these ingredients from your local spice store. Don't buy the huge packets as you may never get through them. Get small amounts and keep them in airtight containers.

All the other ingredients will have to be bought fresh for specific dishes. We recommend that you use a thick-based pot or frying pan for all dishes (ideally a thawa, see below) as this will ensure an even distribution of heat and help prevent the food from burning.

Equipment

If possible try to source the items below. The results will be much better.

THAWA

A slightly concave frying pan or griddle, usually made of cast iron, this is used for cooking chapatis or parathas. An ordinary heavy-duty, thick-based frying pan can be used as a substitute.

DEEP FAT FRYER

Ideally, you will need something like this for pakoras and fritters. If you can't stretch to one (and there are some very good fryers which have filter-covers which remove odours) then go with a good, deep saucepan with a thick base. Remember that hot fat is very dangerous, so be careful!

SKEWERS

Wooden skewers are the best type of skewers to use for kebabs. You can use metal skewers if you like, but allow them to cool before threading the next batch onto them.

Tips and hints

PREPARING AND COOKING THE FOOD

• Cooking an Indian meal is not at all difficult. Common sense is the best guide to follow in preparing a variety of dishes. Spice mixing when cooking a dish is a skill that can be learnt through care and imagination. The taste given to a dish depends on the combination of spices used.

• When cooking for others, consider the preferences of your friends. Someone who doesn't normally eat Indian food can be put off by something that is too hot. Remember, too, that many people don't like the taste of coriander.

- All the vegetables, meat and chicken should generally be the same size. This will help to ensure even cooking.

- During cooking, food may start sticking to the pan. If this happens, add a little water. Using a thick-based pot ought to help prevent sticking and burning.

- Because ginger and garlic are used in a lot of curries, it's a good idea to take about 300g (10oz) of each one, and soak them separately in water overnight (this makes them easier to peel). The next day peel and grind them separately in a food processor, adding a little water to make a pulp. The pulps can be stored in airtight containers in the fridge for 3-4 weeks. Alternatively, pour the individual pulps in ice cube trays and freeze, and use as and when required.

- Coriander is not always easy to buy fresh. You can buy it in large quantities when it is in season, finely chop and freeze in small batches in food bags for later use.

- Meal planning: Diversity and balance are the key words in planning an Indian meal. Flavours should blend with each other to create a spread that is pleasing to all the senses. Indian dishes are ideal for group eating because, rather than preparing one dish per person, several are presented to share with everyone. Make sure that the dishes compliment one another. Think in terms of spicy, medium, mild, dry and moist dishes, as well as a selection of meat, poultry, seafood and vegetarian dishes.

- Always allow the necessary time for cooking, planning and marinading the food. If you start to rush things along, disaster could ensue and you'll end up ordering from the local carry out.

2. STARTERS AND SNACKS

Spicy Potato Fritters

These potato fritters are deep fried and the batter is made with chickpea flour. They can be served as starters, as a snack with dips, as finger food at parties and as a side dish with any main curry.

You need to be careful – these are addictive and you'll end up fighting over them!

PREPARATION
20 minutes

COOKING TIME
5-7 mins per batch

OIL TEMP
160-180°C

INGREDIENTS

75g (3oz) chickpea flour, sieved
Pinch of baking powder
1 tsp salt or to taste
1 tsp ground cumin
1 tsp ground coriander
1/2 tsp red chilli powder
1/2 tsp turmeric powder
1/2 tsp garlic paste
1/2 tsp ginger paste
125 ml (4fl oz) water
500g (1lb) medium sized potatoes,
peeled and cut into 1/2 cm (1/4-inch) thick slices
Oil for deep frying

METHOD

- Sift the chickpea flour and baking powder into a large bowl and mix in the salt, spices, garlic and ginger. Add the water to make a smooth batter, beat well and then set aside.
- Add the potatoes to the chickpea paste and mix until they are fully coated.
- Heat the oil over a medium heat and dip in as many potato slices as the pan will hold in a single layer and fry them until golden brown (5-7 minutes per batch).
- Drain on kitchen paper.
- Continue to batch fry until the potatoes are finished.
- Serve hot, with tomato ketchup, yoghurt dip or a chutney of your choice.

Cauliflower Pakoras

This is a standard favourite in Scotland. Pakora comes in many forms: plain, mushroom, chicken, fish, tomato, mixed vegetable. Cauliflower is still one of the most popular, especially in Glasgow. Pakoras aren't so popular in Indian restaurants in England, where onion bhajias are more likely to be found.

PREPARATION
20 minutes

COOKING TIME
5-7 mins per batch

OIL TEMP
160-180°C

INGREDIENTS

125g (5oz) chickpea flour, sieved

Pinch of baking powder

1/2 tsp salt or to taste

1 tsp ground cumin

1 tsp ground coriander

1/2 tsp red chilli powder

1/2 tsp garlic paste

1/2 tsp ginger paste

150 ml (5fl oz) water

1 medium sized cauliflower, cut into 2.5cm (1-inch) florets

1 tsp lemon juice

oil for deep frying

METHOD

• Sift the chickpea flour and baking powder into a large bowl and mix thoroughly. Add salt, spices, garlic and ginger. Add the water to make a smooth batter, beat well and then set aside.

• Add the cauliflower to the chickpea paste and mix well, fully coating the florets.

• Heat the oil over a medium heat and dip in a few florets at a time. Allow to deep fry until golden brown. Don't allow them to brown too much or too quickly as this just burns the coating and does not cook the florets inside.

• Drain on kitchen paper.

• Continue to batch fry until the mixture is finished.

• Serve hot with dips of your choice.

Vegetable Pakoras

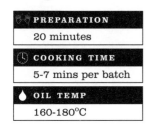

PREPARATION
20 minutes

COOKING TIME
5-7 mins per batch

OIL TEMP
160-180°C

INGREDIENTS

200g (7oz) chickpea flour, sieved

1 tsp salt or to taste

1 tsp cumin seeds

½ tsp garam masala

½ tsp red chilli powder

1 tsp fenugreek leaves

1 tsp garlic pulp

1 medium sized onion, chopped

1 small potato peeled and finely chopped

1 sprig of fresh coriander, finely chopped

2 fresh spinach leaves, finely chopped

125-150ml (4-5fl oz) water

Oil for deep frying

METHOD

- Sift the chickpea flour into a large bowl, then mix in the salt, spices, garlic, onion and vegetables. Add the water to make a smooth but thick batter.
- Heat the oil over a medium heat in deep-fat fryer.
- Using a tablespoon, scoop up a ball of the mixture and dip in as many of these as the pan will hold in a single layer. Fry them until golden brown (6-8 minutes per batch).
- Drain on kitchen paper.
- Continue to batch fry until mixture is finished.
- Serve hot with tomato ketchup, yoghurt dip or a chutney of your choice.

Onion Bhajias

PREPARATION
20 minutes

COOKING TIME
6-8 mins per batch

OIL TEMP
160-180°C

INGREDIENTS

200g (6oz) chickpea flour, sieved

Pinch of baking powder

1 tsp salt

1 tsp red chilli powder

1 tsp ground cumin

1 tsp ground coriander

7 fresh green chillies, finely chopped (optional)

1 tsp garlic pulp

1 sprig of fresh coriander leaves, finely chopped

1 tsp lemon juice

2 large onions peeled,

halved and cut to form

thin crescent-shaped slices

Oil for deep-frying

175ml (6fl oz) water

METHOD

- Sift the flour and the baking powder into a large bowl. Add the salt, spices, garlic and freshly chopped coriander leaves, and mix well.
- Add the onions and mix thoroughly.
- Add the lemon juice then gradually add the water and keep mixing until a soft but thick batter is formed and the onions are well coated.
- Before cooking the bhajias, test that the oil temperature is correct by dropping a tiny amount of batter into the oil. If it floats up to the surface immediately, but does not turn brown, the oil is at the correct temperature.
- Using a tablespoon, scoop up a ball of the mixture and dip in as many of these as the pan will hold in a single layer. Fry them until golden brown (6-8 minutes per batch).
- Drain on kitchen paper.
- Continue to batch fry until mixture is finished.
- Serve with dips of your choice.

Minced Lamb Kebabs
(Barbecue or Grill)

When you are buying the mince ask for it to be run through the mincer twice to make it finer.

The skewered kebab is another type of dish altogether, although most Westerners assume that all kebabs are skewered.

INGREDIENTS

PREPARATION
20 minutes

COOKING TIME
6-8 minutes

OIL TEMP
160-180°C

8 green chillies finely chopped

6 black peppercorns

4 cloves

3 green cardamoms

1 sprig of fresh coriander leaves, finely chopped

$\frac{1}{2}$ tsp of freshly chopped or bottled mint

500g (1lb) minced lamb

1 small onion, very finely chopped

1 egg yolk

1 tsp salt

$\frac{1}{4}$ tsp red chilli powder

$\frac{3}{4}$ tsp ginger pulp

1 tsp garlic pulp

Juice of half a lemon

METHOD

- In a blender of coffee grinder, grind the green chillies, black peppercorns, cloves, green cardamoms, coriander and mint and blend this to a smooth paste, adding a little water if necessary.
- Transfer the mixture to a large bowl, adding the meat, onion, egg yolk, salt, red chilli powder, garlic, ginger and lemon juice and knead the mixture until all the ingredients are mixed thoroughly.
- Set the mixture aside for 10-15 minutes as this will allow the egg to bind the mixture together.
- Break the mixture into small, golf ball sized pieces, and flatten them in the palm of your hand using the fingers of your other hand to pat them flat.
- Cook over a barbecue or under a grill. Turn the kebabs regularly to ensure even cooking throughout.
- Serve with cucumber and mint raita (p23), a mixed green salad and bread of your choice.

3. SAUCES AND CHUTNEYS

Spiced Onions

These chunky spiced onions are really popular as a starter with poppadoms. Some restaurant owners are more generous than others and give free spiced onions and poppadoms before taking your order. Nice chaps!

PREPARATION
6-7 minutes plus 30 minutes refrigeration

INGREDIENTS

2 large onions, finely chopped

3 tbsp tomato ketchup

1 tbsp tomato paste

$\frac{1}{2}$ tsp mint sauce

$\frac{1}{2}$ tsp red chilli powder

$\frac{1}{4}$ tsp salt or to taste

1 tsp lemon juice

METHOD

- Place the onions in a bowl. Add the tomato ketchup, tomato paste, mint sauce, red chilli powder, salt and lemon juice and mix well together.
- Cover and refrigerate for 30 minutes before serving.

Cucumber and Mint Raita

Raitas involve no cooking. This raita is rather cooling, very appetising and it is good as an accompaniment. You don't have to have Indian food to have raita – it can be used as a salad sauce or eaten with celery sticks.

PREPARATION
6-7 minutes

INGREDIENTS

250ml (8fl oz) plain, unsweetened yoghurt

1/4 cucumber, grated or chopped

1/4 tsp salt

1/2 tsp ground black pepper

1 tsp mint sauce

1/4 tsp red chilli powder

1 sprig of fresh coriander leaves

METHOD

- Beat the natural yoghurt and place in a serving bowl
- Add in the other ingredients and mix well.
- Finely chop the coriander and garnish
- Keep in fridge before serving.

Mint Chutney

Raw onion and mint often accompany an Indian meal. You can make it hotter by adding a couple of chopped green chillies. Use red onions to add colour.

PREPARATION

6-7 minutes plus
30 minutes
refrigeration

INGREDIENTS

2 medium sized onions (preferably red), finely chopped

1 tsp red chilli powder

1 tsp ground black pepper

1 tsp salt

4 sprigs fresh mint, finely chopped

1 tbsp vinegar

3 tbsp plain, unsweetened yoghurt

2 green chillies, finely chopped (optional)

METHOD

• Place the onions in a bowl. Add the red chilli powder, ground black pepper, salt, fresh mint, vinegar, green chillies (if using) and the yoghurt and mix well together.

• Cover with a lid and refrigerate for 30 minutes before serving.

Hot Sweet Dip

A contrast to other savoury dips and a good way to soothe that 'chilli sensation'. Many people will have both sweet and savoury dips at the table together. Add extra sugar or honey to increase the sweetness of this dip. It is good poured onto a hot naan or paratha as a snack.

PREPARATION
2-3 minutes

INGREDIENTS

125ml (4fl oz) olive oil

60ml (2fl oz) white vinegar

60ml (2fl oz) sweet chilli sauce

1 tsp sugar

METHOD

• Combine all the ingredients in a jar, shake well and serve.

Curried French Dip

This is one we invented ourselves – it has a distinctive flavour not found in an ordinary Indian restaurant. After preparing the dips in this book, you'll probably be able to create some of your own.

PREPARATION
2-3 minutes

INGREDIENTS

125ml (4fl oz) olive oil

60ml (2fl oz) white vinegar

1 tsp curry powder

$\frac{1}{2}$ tsp red chilli powder

1 sprig of fresh coriander, finely chopped

2 green shallots, finely chopped

METHOD

• Combine the ingredients in a jar, shake well and serve.

Spicy Corn and Herb Dip

One for the barbecue table when you have friends round, this dip is not often seen in Indian restaurants. You can use this with grilled chicken or a piece of barbecued beef.

PREPARATION
5-6 minutes

INGREDIENTS

100g (4oz) mayonnaise

100g (4fl oz) soured cream

300g (10oz) can creamed corn

1 tbsp lemon juice

1 tbsp sweet chilli sauce

$\frac{1}{2}$ tsp garam masala

$\frac{1}{2}$ tsp garlic pulp

1 sprig of fresh parsley, finely chopped

1 sprig of fresh chives, finely chopped

METHOD

• Combine all the ingredients in a bowl, mix well and serve.

4. MAIN MEAT DISHES

Chicken Curry

Since the early sixties, restaurant reputations have been built on the quality of the house chicken curry. It remains among the top dishes alongside Chicken Bhuna, Chicken Tikka Masala and Lamb Bhuna.

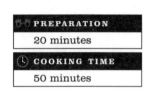

PREPARATION
20 minutes

COOKING TIME
50 minutes

INGREDIENTS

9 tbsp oil

2 medium sized onions, chopped

1 x 2.5cm (1-inch) cinnamon stick

4 cloves

3 green cardamoms

2 bay leaves

500g (1lb) boned skinless chicken cut into 2.5cm (1-inch) cubes

1 tbsp ginger pulp

1 tbsp garlic pulp

2 tomatoes quartered

1 tbsp tomato paste

1 tsp red chilli powder

1 tsp turmeric powder

½ tsp salt

½ tsp ground cumin

300ml (10fl oz) warm water

½ tsp garam masala

2 sprigs of fresh coriander leaves, finely chopped

METHOD

• Heat the oil over a medium heat in a saucepan, add onions and gently fry until soft.

• Stir in the cinnamon stick, cloves, cardamoms and bay leaves and fry for a further 2 minutes.

• Add the chicken, ginger, garlic and tomatoes and fry for a further 3 minutes.

• Stir in the tomato paste, chilli powder, turmeric, salt and cumin and then fry for a further 2 minutes.

• Lower the temperature, add the warm water and part-cover the saucepan with a lid, leaving a half-inch gap. Cook for about 40 minutes, stirring occasionally.

• Stir in the garam masala and garnish with chopped fresh coriander.

• Serve with bay fried rice (p84) and chapatis (p80).

Chicken Ceylonese Korma

Korma dishes are generally prepared with fresh cream, nuts and mild spices and come in many variations. The Ceylonese korma is often preferred by those who like a mild tasting curry. Not for the weight watcher – don't blame us if you pile on the pounds.

PREPARATION

20 minutes plus
3 hours for
marinading

COOKING TIME

1 hour

INGREDIENTS

1 tbsp garlic pulp

1 tsp ginger pulp

2 red chillies

60ml (2fl oz) water

125g (4oz) plain
unsweetened yoghurt

1 tsp salt

1.3 kg (3lb) boneless, skinless
chicken, cut into 2.5cm (1-inch) cubes

2 medium sized onions, coarsely chopped

2 tbsp tomato paste

4 tbsp cooking oil

1 tsp turmeric powder

1 tsp garam masala

75g (3oz) creamed coconut,
cut into small pieces

125ml (4fl oz) single cream

2 tsp ground cashew nuts

25g (1oz) flaked almonds

METHOD

- Place the garlic, ginger, red chillies and around 25 ml of water in a food processor and liquidise to a smooth paste.
- Mix this paste with the yoghurt and salt and place in a large bowl. Blend with a whisk.
- Add the chicken, and ensure the pieces are well coated by the mixture.
- Cover with cling film and set aside for 3 hours to marinade.
- Place 1 chopped onion, tomato paste and around 25ml of water in a food processor and liquidise to a pulp.
- Heat the oil over a medium heat in a saucepan and fry the other chopped onion until soft.
- Stir in the turmeric powder, garam masala and add the chicken with the marinade. Continue to fry for around 5 minutes, stirring constantly.
- Add the liquidised onion pulp and continue to fry on a low to medium heat for around 10 minutes, stirring occasionally.
- Stir in the remaining water and creamed coconut. Bring to the boil and stir until the coconut is dissolved.
- Add in the single cream and give the dish a good stir. Then stir in the ground cashew nuts.
- Reduce the heat to low and part-cover the saucepan with a lid, leaving a half-inch gap. Simmer for about 40 minutes, stirring occasionally.
- To finish, sprinkle in the flaked almonds, and serve with boiled rice.

Chicken Bazzigar

This dish is prepared in a slightly spiced sauce with green peppers, mushrooms and pineapples. This is all blended with warm spices and gives an excellent dish of medium to slightly hot strength. More of a summer dish than a winter one.

PREPARATION
20-25 minutes

COOKING TIME
1 hour

INGREDIENTS

10 tbsp of oil

1 large onion, chopped

1 tsp cumin seeds

500g (1lb) boned skinless chicken cut into 2.5cm (1-inch) cubes

2 tomatoes quartered

1 tsp red chilli powder

1 tsp turmeric powder

1 tsp ginger pulp

1 tsp garlic pulp

1 tbsp medium curry paste

1 tbsp tomato paste

2 sprigs of fresh coriander leaves, finely chopped

1 tsp salt

250ml (8fl oz) warm water

1 green chilli, finely chopped

1 green pepper, cored, deseeded and chopped

6 button mushrooms, chopped

1 tsp fenugreek leaves

8 pineapple chunks

1 tsp garam masala

METHOD

• Heat the oil over a medium heat in a saucepan and fry the onion gently until soft. Add the cumin seeds and fry for a further 2 minutes or until they start to crackle.

• Add the chicken and tomatoes and fry for a further 3-4 minutes. Stir in the red chilli powder, turmeric powder, ginger, garlic, curry paste, tomato paste, half the coriander, salt and the warm water and cook for 5 minutes, giving the saucepan a right good stir.

• Lower the heat slightly and add the green chilli and green pepper and cook for 20 minutes, stirring occasionally. Add the mushrooms, fenugreek leaves and pineapple chunks and part-cover the saucepan with a lid, leaving a half-inch gap.

• Cook for around 30 minutes, checking and stirring occasionally. Stir in the garam masala and garnish with the remaining coriander on top.

• Serve with matter pilau (see p83).

Chicken Do-Piazza

This is an easy dish to prepare. Do-Piazza means two onions – this dish is slightly heavier on the onions than is usual.

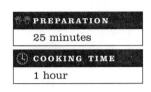

PREPARATION
25 minutes

COOKING TIME
1 hour

INGREDIENTS

7 tbsp of oil

2 large onions, thinly chopped

2.5cm (1-inch) cinnamon stick

4 cloves

3 green cardamoms

2 bay leaves

750g (1.5lb) boned skinless chicken cut into 2.5cm (1-inch) cubes

1 tbsp ginger pulp

1 tbsp garlic pulp

2 tomatoes quartered

1 tsp red chilli powder

1 tsp turmeric powder

1 tsp salt

1 tsp ground cumin

300ml (10fl oz) warm water

1 tsp garam masala

2 sprigs of fresh coriander leaves, finely chopped

METHOD

- Heat 4 tbsp of the oil (60ml) in a saucepan, fry 1 onion until soft.
- Stir in the cinnamon stick, cloves, cardamoms and bay leaves and fry for a further 2 minutes.
- Add the chicken, ginger, garlic and tomatoes and fry for a further 3 minutes.
- Stir in the chilli powder, turmeric, salt and ground cumin and then fry for a further 2 minutes. Lower the heat, add the warm water and part-cover the saucepan with a lid, leaving a half-inch gap, and cook for about 40 minutes, stirring occasionally.
- In a separate pan, heat the remaining 3 tablespoons of oil (45ml) in a saucepan, add the other onion, and fry until golden brown.
- Add this mixture to the main saucepan, stir in and sprinkle in the garam masala.
- Garnish with chopped fresh coriander and serve with boiled rice and puris (see p81).

Chicken Saag
Chicken with Spinach (Murgh aur Palak)

This is one of our favourite dishes. It is a delicious combination of cumin, coriander and chillies. People who don't like spinach are often converted after trying this dish.

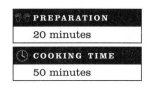

PREPARATION
20 minutes

COOKING TIME
50 minutes

INGREDIENTS

4 tbsp of oil

2 medium sized onions, finely chopped

1/2 tsp cumin seeds

1/2 tsp fennel seeds

4 cloves

2 green chillies finely chopped

2 bay leaves

750g (1.5 lb) boned skinless chicken cut into 2.5cm (1-inch) cubes

2 tomatoes quartered

1 tbsp ginger pulp

1 tbsp garlic pulp

1/2 tsp red chilli powder

1 tsp turmeric powder

1 tsp salt

2 sprigs of fresh coriander leaves, finely chopped

125ml (4fl oz) warm water

425g (14oz) canned spinach, drained,

or fresh spinach, washed and chopped

1/2 tsp garam masala

METHOD

- Heat the oil in a saucepan, then add the onions, frying them gently until soft.
- Stir in the cumin, fennel, cloves, green chillies and bay leaves and fry for a further 2 minutes.
- Add the chicken, tomatoes, ginger and garlic and stir-fry for a further 3 minutes. Stir in the chilli powder, turmeric, salt, half the fresh coriander and then fry for a further 2 minutes.
- Lower the heat, add the warm water and part-cover the saucepan with a lid, leaving a half-inch gap. Cook for about 15 minutes, checking and stirring occasionally.
- Add the canned or chopped fresh spinach and cook for a further 25 minutes, stirring occasionally.
- Stir in the garam masala and garnish with the remaining fresh coriander on top. Serve with chapatis (se p80).

Kofte ka Salan
(Curried Meatballs)

When you are buying the mince ask for it to be run through the mincer twice to make it finer. This will allow the ingredients to mix with ease and stay together while cooking. There's not a lot of sauce with this dish as it is very rich in taste.

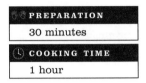

PREPARATION
30 minutes

COOKING TIME
1 hour

METHOD

- Put the mince in a large bowl and add the ginger, garlic, cumin, salt and red chilli powder. Mix the ingredients thoroughly and knead the mince until the whole mixture is smooth.
- Break the mixture into small, golf ball sized pieces, and roll into balls between the palms of your hands.
- To make the sauce, heat the oil on a medium heat in a large saucepan and fry the onion until light brown. Add the green cardamoms, black cardamom and cloves and fry for 2 minutes.
- Lower the heat and stir in the ginger, garlic, red chilli powder, turmeric powder, garam masala and tomato paste and gently fry for a further minute. Add the yoghurt and salt and cook until the mixture is dry or the oil rises to the surface. Stir in the water, adjust the heat back to medium, cover and cook for 10 minutes.
- Gently add the koftas, 1 at a time, to the sauce.
- Partially cover the saucepan and simmer gently for 40-45 minutes.
- If you feel that the sauce is too thick, add a little water and mix through.
- Garnish with the freshly chopped coriander and serve with cucumber and mint raita (see p23) and boiled rice.

INGREDIENTS

For the meatballs:
500g (1lb) lean mince, lamb or beef
1/2 tsp ginger pulp
1 tsp garlic pulp
1 tsp ground cumin
1/2 tsp salt
1/2 tsp red chilli powder

For the sauce:
4 tbsp of oil
1 large onion, chopped
2 green cardamoms
1 black cardamom
4 cloves
1 tsp ginger pulp
1 tsp garlic pulp
1/2 tsp red chilli powder
1 tsp turmeric powder
1/2 tsp garam masala
2 tbsp tomato paste
150ml (5fl oz) plain, unsweetened yoghurt
1 tsp salt
300ml (10fl oz) warm water
1 sprig of fresh coriander, finely chopped

Bhoona Gosht
(Fried Lamb)

The word 'Bhoon' translated means 'fry' and the word 'Gosht' means 'meat'. Bhoona Gosht is a method of cooking lamb fairly quickly using the minimum amount of moisture.
It's better to use lamb, rather than mutton, which takes twice as long to cook.

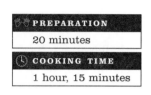

PREPARATION
20 minutes

COOKING TIME
1 hour, 15 minutes

INGREDIENTS

1kg (2.2lbs) leg or shoulder of lamb

6 tbsp of cooking oil

1 fairly large onion, chopped

1 tbsp ginger pulp

2 tbsp garlic pulp

1 tsp red chilli powder

1 tsp turmeric powder

1 tsp ground coriander

1 tsp ground cumin

11 green cardamoms

2 black cardamoms

6 cloves

3 bay leaves

3 medium sized tomatoes, quartered

1 tsp salt

½ tsp of fenugreek leaves

2-3 sprigs of fresh coriander leaves, finely chopped

450ml (15fl oz) warm water

1 tsp garam masala

METHOD

- Trim off any excess fat from the lamb and cut into 2.5cm (1-inch) cubes.
- Heat the oil over a medium heat and fry the onion until soft. Add the ginger and garlic, stir-frying for around 1-2 minutes. Add the red chilli powder, ground turmeric, ground coriander, ground cumin, green cardamoms, black cardamoms, cloves, bay leaves, tomatoes, the meat and salt.
- Turn the heat up high and fry the meat for 2-3 minutes, stirring continuously to avoid the ingredients sticking to the base of the pan. Reduce the heat to medium and add the fenugreek leaves and half of the coriander leaves.
- Fry for a further 5 minutes, stirring frequently. The texture of the meat should now look fairly dry.
- Add the warm water and bring to the boil, cover and simmer for around 50-60 minutes or until the meat is tender.
- Stir in the garam masala and the remaining coriander and serve with spiced onions (p22) and chapatis (p80).

Lamb with Spinach

Lamb and spinach are a delicious combination. We recommend you use fresh spinach for this recipe although you can use frozen or canned spinach. Be careful not to add more spinach than is recommended as it can overwhelm the other flavours in the dish.

PREPARATION
20 minutes

COOKING TIME
1 hour, 20 minutes

INGREDIENTS

4 tbsp of cooking oil

1 medium sized onion, chopped

1 tsp ginger pulp

1 tbsp garlic pulp

1 tsp red chilli powder

1 tsp ground cumin

1 tsp ground coriander

3 tomatoes, skinned and roughly chopped

1 tsp turmeric powder

1 tsp salt

500g (1lb) lamb, cut into small cubes

300ml (10fl oz) warm water

1kg (2.2lb) spinach, trimmed and washed

or 2 x 225g (2 x 8oz) frozen leaf spinach, thawed and chopped

METHOD

- Heat the oil in a large saucepan and fry the onion until light brown. Add the ginger, garlic, red chilli powder, cumin powder and coriander powder and gently fry for 2 to 3 minutes.
- Add the tomatoes, turmeric powder and salt. Continue to fry gently for 7 to 8 minutes.
- Add the meat and cook for 10 minutes, or until it is dry.
- Add the warm water, part-cover the saucepan with a lid, leaving a half-inch gap, and cook for about 50 minutes, checking and stirring occasionally.
- After about 30 minutes, when the sauce has reduced by half, stir in the spinach, cover and simmer gently for the remaining 20 minutes.
- Serve as a main dish with boiled rice or bread of your choice.

Shahi Spring Lamb Korma

If possible, use spring lamb for this dish. Not only is it more tender than ordinary lamb, but it also cuts down on the cooking time. This curry makes an excellent dinner party centrepiece and is well suited to those who don't like too much spice.

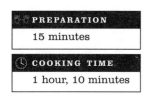

PREPARATION
15 minutes

COOKING TIME
1 hour, 10 minutes

INGREDIENTS

4 tbsp of cooking oil

2 medium sized onions, finely chopped

2 bay leaves

3 green cardamoms

500g (1lb) spring lamb, cut into small cubes

½ tsp fennel seeds

2 tsp coconut powder

1 tsp garam masala

1 tsp coriander powder

½ tsp red chilli powder

1 tsp ginger pulp

1 tsp garlic pulp

1 tsp salt

75ml (3oz) plain, unsweetened yoghurt

250ml (8fl oz) warm water

25g (1oz) sultanas

150ml (5fl oz) cream

1 large pinch saffron

8 cashew nuts

1 sprig of fresh coriander, finely chopped

METHOD

- Heat the oil in a large saucepan over a medium heat and gently fry the onions, bay leaves and cardamoms until light brown. Remove from the heat and set aside.
- In a large bowl add the lamb, fennel seeds, coconut powder, garam masala, coriander powder, red chilli powder, ginger, garlic, salt and yoghurt and mix with your hands.
- Return the saucepan to the heat and reheat the onion mixture for about 2 minutes.
- Add the lamb mixture to the saucepan and cook for about 5 minutes, stirring occasionally. Add the water and lower the heat, part-cover the saucepan with a lid, leaving a half-inch gap, and cook for 40-45 minutes, checking and stirring occasionally to see that the sauce has reduced.
- Stir in the cream, sultanas, saffron and cashew nuts and continue to cook for 10-15 minutes.
- Transfer to a serving dish, garnish with the freshly chopped coriander and serve with matter pilau (p83) and mint chutney (p24).

Lamb Chops

This is a speciality in Asian households and one of our favourite dishes. It is prepared in a masala sauce and can be adapted as required in terms of texture and the strength of spice.

The lamb chops are flattened with a wooden mallet so the meat is prepared for shallow frying.

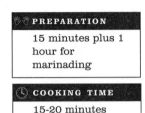

PREPARATION

15 minutes plus 1 hour for marinading

COOKING TIME

15-20 minutes

INGREDIENTS

6 lamb chops, flattened with a wooden mallet

For the masala sauce:

3/4 tsp red chilli powder

1/2 tsp turmeric powder

1/2 tsp black pepper

1/2 tsp ground cumin

1/2 tsp garlic pulp

1/4 tsp salt

2.5 ml vinegar

Juice of half a lemon

Oil for shallow frying

METHOD

- Stir all the sauce ingredients together in a bowl to form a sauce.
- Rub the sauce all over the chops on both sides and leave to marinade for an hour.
- Heat the oil in a large frying pan and shallow fry the lamb on each side until thoroughly cooked.
- Serve with chapatis (p80), lemon slices and a salad of your choice.

Beef Pasanda

The key to making this dish is to cut the meat into thin strips and begin the preparations the night before. Rump or sirloin steak with fat removed should be used as frying steak is often too thin.

PREPARATION

30 minutes plus marinading overnight

COOKING TIME

1 hour, 20 minutes

INGREDIENTS

750g (1.5lb) beef, cut into 2.5cm (1-inch) strips

For the marinade:

150ml (5fl oz) plain unsweetened yoghurt

1 tbsp garlic pulp

1 tsp ginger pulp

1 tsp salt

1 tsp coriander powder

1 tsp cumin powder

Juice of 1 lemon

75g (3oz) unsalted butter

2 medium sized onions, finely chopped

25g (1oz) ground almonds

1 tsp turmeric powder

1/2 tsp red chilli powder

1 green chilli deseeded, and finely chopped

125ml (4fl oz) warm water

150ml (5fl oz) single cream

12.5g (1/2 oz) almond flakes

METHOD

- Put the strips of beef in a large bowl, add the yoghurt, garlic, ginger, salt, coriander powder, cumin and lemon juice. Mix well together, cover and leave to marinade overnight.
- Heat the butter over a medium heat in a large saucepan and fry the onions gently until light brown.
- Add the marinaded beef and fry until it changes colour. Add the turmeric and red chilli powder, almonds and green chilli and continue to fry for 4-5 minutes, stirring frequently.
- Lower the heat, add the warm water, part-cover the saucepan with a lid, leaving a half-inch gap, and simmer for about 50 minutes checking and stirring occasionally.
- Add the cream and let it all simmer uncovered for around 10 minutes.
- Stir in the garam masala, put the pasanda into a serving dish and sprinkle the almond flakes on top. Serve with boiled rice.

Keema Matter
(Mince and Peas)

Lean mince is combined with garden peas to make this delicious dish that is popular all over India and Pakistan.

Keema is also used to fill samosas and is usually cooked until dry. Buy only the leanest steak or lamb mince to get the best results.

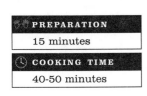

PREPARATION
15 minutes

COOKING TIME
40-50 minutes

INGREDIENTS

4 tbsp of cooking oil

1 onion, finely chopped

1 tsp cumin seeds

2 black cardamoms

4 small green cardamoms

1 bay leaf

1 tsp ginger pulp

1 tbsp garlic pulp

1 tsp tomato paste

2 tomatoes quartered

500g (1 lb) lean steak or lamb mince

1 tsp red chilli powder

$\frac{1}{2}$ tsp turmeric powder

125 ml (4fl oz) warm water

1 tsp salt

$\frac{1}{2}$ tsp tsp fenugreek leaves

175g (6 oz) frozen garden peas (thawed)

$\frac{1}{2}$ tsp garam masala

2 sprigs of fresh coriander leaves, finely chopped

METHOD

- Heat the oil in a saucepan, and add the finely chopped onion. Fry until soft, then stir in the cumin seds, cardamoms and bay leaf and fry for another 3-4 minutes.
- Add the ginger, garlic, tomato paste and the quartered tomatoes and continue frying gently for 1 minute. Add the mince and sprinkle in the red chilli powder, turmeric and continue stir-frying for 7-10 minutes.
- Add the warm water, salt and fenugreek leaves, cover the pan and simmer for 15 minutes.
- Add the thawed peas and simmer for a further 15 minutes.
- Finally, stir in the garam masala and garnish with the coriander leaves.
- Serve with mint chutney (p24), chapatis (p80) and mango pickle.

5. VEGETARIAN DISHES

Mixed Vegetable Curry

A mixed vegetable curry is exactly what it says it is – a variety of seasonal vegetables that are cooked together and flavoured with ground spices. Chopped coriander leaves are added towards the end of cooking this dish to enhance the flavour. Use any combination of vegetables you want. If you are using root vegetables – potatoes or carrots – par-boil them beforehand to ensure they are fully cooked.

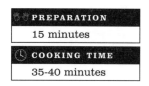

PREPARATION
15 minutes

COOKING TIME
35-40 minutes

METHOD

- Heat the oil in a saucepan, and fry the onion until lightly brown.
- Add the cumin seeds and continue to fry until the onions go light brown and the cumin seeds start to crackle.
- Add the red chilli powder, black pepper, ground coriander, turmeric, salt, ginger, garlic, cloves, and tomato paste and stir for around 1 minute.
- Stir the vegetables gently into the spicy sauce, add the chopped tomatoes, sprinkle in the fenugreek leaves and warm water. Increase the heat, bring to the boil, cover and cook gently for 7-10 minutes.
- Add the green chillies, coriander, and garam masala, stir in well and cook gently for a further 10 minutes or until the vegetables are tender.
- Serve as a side dish, or as a main dish with rice or bread of your choice.

INGREDIENTS

4 tbsp of oil

1 medium sized onion, chopped

1 tsp cumin seeds

1 tsp red chilli powder

1 tsp ground coriander

1/2 tsp turmeric powder

1 tsp salt

1 tsp ginger pulp

1 tsp garlic pulp

3 garlic cloves

1 tsp tomato paste

500g (1lb) of mixed vegetables of your choice (potatoes, carrots, cauliflower, peas)

2 tomatoes peeled and diced

1 pinch of fenugreek leaves

125ml (4 fl oz) of warm water

2 green chillies de-seeded, and finely chopped

2 sprigs of fresh coriander leaves, finely chopped

1 tsp garam masala

1/2 tsp black pepper

Mushroom Bhoona
(Dry Mushroom Curry)

Mushrooms were not a big hit in our house when we were young and we can't ever remember having them cooked at home. They are now widely used in Indian cooking, with delicious results.

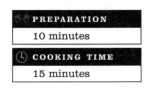

PREPARATION
10 minutes

COOKING TIME
15 minutes

INGREDIENTS

4 tbsp of oil

1 medium sized onion, chopped

1 tsp ginger pulp

1 tsp garlic pulp

$\frac{1}{2}$ tsp turmeric powder

$\frac{1}{2}$ tsp red chilli powder

$\frac{1}{2}$ tsp coriander powder

1 tsp ground cumin

$\frac{1}{2}$ tsp salt

1 tbsp tomato paste

225g (8oz) mushrooms chopped

60ml (2fl oz) warm water

1 sprig of fresh coriander, finely chopped

METHOD

- Heat the oil in a saucepan, and fry the onion until light brown.
- Lower the heat and add the ginger, garlic, turmeric powder, chilli powder, coriander powder and ground cumin and stir for 2-3 minutes.
- Add the salt and tomato paste and continue to stir-fry for 2 minutes.
- Stir in the warm water and add the mushrooms. Cover the saucepan and simmer for 7-8 minutes, stir once.
- Sprinkle in the coriander and serve as a side or main dish with plain unsweetened yoghurt and chapatis (p80).

Bhindi Bhaji
(Okra)

Okra (also known as lady fingers) is available throughout the world, although it is not often used for western cooking. When buying okra, make sure it's fresh, and avoid any that are starting to turn soft and black.

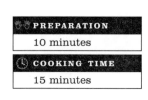

PREPARATION
10 minutes

COOKING TIME
15 minutes

INGREDIENTS

500g (1lb) okra

3 tbsp of oil

1 medium sized onion, chopped

1 tsp chilli powder

1 tsp ground cumin

1 tsp garam masala

$\frac{1}{2}$ tsp black pepper

$\frac{1}{2}$ tsp turmeric powder

1 tsp salt

1 sprig of fresh coriander, finely chopped

METHOD

- Prepare the okra by cutting away the stalk and tail of each one, and chop them into 1cm ($\frac{1}{2}$-inch) lengths.
- Heat the oil in a saucepan and fry the onion until light brown.
- Add the red chilli powder, ground cumin, garam masala, black pepper and turmeric powder and stir-fry for 1 minute.
- Add the Okra and salt, cover the saucepan and simmer for around 10 minutes.
- If the mixture becomes too dry during cooking add a little water.
- Stir in the coriander and serve as a side, or main dish with cucumber and mint raita (p23) and puris (p81).

Aloo Gobi
(Cauliflower Curry)

A very popular dish among vegetarians, which, if made properly, has a superb taste and is ideal as a side dish.

This is drier than other dishes, although wholesome and refreshing, and is best served with fresh bread. If you have friends that don't like cauliflower, ask them to try this and they might be converted.

PREPARATION
10 minutes

COOKING TIME
20-22 minutes

INGREDIENTS

1 medium sized cauliflower

4 tbsp of oil

1 medium sized onion, finely chopped

1 tsp red chilli powder

1 tsp ginger pulp

1 tsp garlic pulp

1 tsp turmeric powder

1 tsp cumin powder

1 tsp tomato paste

$\frac{1}{2}$ tsp salt

50ml (2oz) warm water

1 tsp lemon juice

1 sprig of fresh coriander, finely chopped

METHOD

- Break the cauliflower into florets, wash, and set aside.
- Heat the oil in a large saucepan and fry the onion until light brown.
- Add the red chilli powder, ginger, garlic, turmeric powder, cumin powder, tomato paste and salt. Stir-fry for 1 minute.
- Add the cauliflower pieces and continue frying for 5 minutes.
- Stir in the warm water, lemon juice and freshly chopped coriander, cover and cook gently for 12-15 minutes.
- Stir twice very gently, otherwise the cauliflower will break into very small pieces.
- Serve with rice or bread of your choice.

6. Seafood

Prawn Curry

This seafood recipe can often be found on the menus of good Indian restaurants worldwide. King, tiger or standard prawns can be used as required.

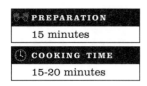

PREPARATION

15 minutes

COOKING TIME

15-20 minutes

METHOD

- Heat the oil in a saucepan, add the onion and fry gently until soft.
- Add the green cardamoms and continue to fry until the onions turn light brown.
- Add the turmeric, cumin, red chilli powder, salt, ginger, garlic and tomato paste and fry for around a minute.
- You are now ready to add the prawns. Stir them gently into the spicy sauce, add the fenugreek leaves, lemon juice and warm water, bring to the boil and gently simmer for around 5 minutes.
- Meanwhile, finely chop the green chilli, add this to the saucepan with the garam masala and stir in gently. Be careful not to stir the prawns too much or some may break, cook gently for a further 5-7 minutes or until the prawns are cooked.
- Put the prawns in a serving dish and garnish with the coriander and a wedge of lemon for decoration.
- Serve with matter pilau (p83) and chapatis (p80).

INGREDIENTS

4 tbsp of oil

1 large onion, chopped

4 green cardamoms

1/2 tsp turmeric powder

1 tsp ground cumin

1 tsp red chilli powder

1/2 tsp salt

1 tsp ginger pulp

1 tsp garlic pulp

1 tsp tomato paste

500g (1 lb) fresh peeled prawns

1 tsp fenugreek leaves

Juice of 1/2 a lemon

60 ml (2 fl oz) warm water

1 green chilli

1/2 tsp garam masala

2 sprigs of fresh coriander leaves, finely chopped

Tandoori Fish

A firm-fleshed white fish is ideal for this dish. The flesh of the fish should be tender and the outside crispy, so we have suggested that you use cod, although any white fish is suitable.

PREPARATION

15 minutes plus 2 hours for refrigeration

COOKING TIME

10 minutes

INGREDIENTS

12 cod fillets

1 tbsp lemon juice

1 tbsp tomato paste

2 tbsp of oil

1 tsp ginger pulp

1 tsp garlic pulp

1 tsp red chilli powder

1 tbsp ground coriander

1 tsp ground cumin

1 tsp salt

1 tsp tandoori paste

2-3 tbsp of water

1 lemon cut into wedges

1 sprig of fresh coriander, finely chopped

METHOD

- Wash the cod fillets and dry thoroughly on absorbent kitchen paper. Rub them with the lemon juice and set aside.
- In a small bowl mix together the tomato paste, oil, ginger, garlic, red chilli powder, ground coriander, ground cumin, salt, tandoori paste and water.
- Pour the mixture over the cod fillets and make sure they are well coated. Cover and leave to marinade in the refrigerator for about 2 hours.
- Place the fillets under a preheated medium grill and cook for 8-10 minutes.
- Garnish with the fresh coriander and lemon wedges and serve immediately.

Mussel Curry

Many people we know use scallops as well as mussels in spice-based cooking and it's becoming more popular as seafood is now available throughout the year. Some Scottish Indian restaurants offer mussels on the menu.

This goes down well with a glass of white wine.

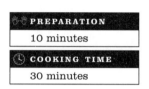

PREPARATION
10 minutes

COOKING TIME
30 minutes

INGREDIENTS

1.8 kg (4lbs) fresh mussels in shells

60ml (2fl oz) cooking oil

1 large onion, finely chopped

3 cloves

1 tsp ginger pulp

1 tsp garlic pulp

1 tsp black pepper

1 tsp ground turmeric

$\frac{1}{2}$ tsp coriander powder

1 tsp fenugreek leaves

1 tsp lemon juice

2 curry leaves (optional)

1 red chilli, finely chopped

1 tsp salt

Warm water

METHOD

- To prepare the mussels wash thoroughly under cold water and pull away any straggly beards that are attached to them. Discard any open mussels at this stage, as they will have died.
- Heat the oil in a large saucepan over a medium heat and fry the onion until soft. Add the cloves, ginger, garlic, black pepper, turmeric powder and coriander powder. Stir well for 2 minutes.
- Add the mussels and cook for 1 minute.
- Add the fenugreek leaves, lemon juice, curry leaves, red chilli and salt, then add just enough warm water to almost cover the mussels. Increase the heat and bring the liquid to the boil.
- Cover the saucepan with a lid and cook over a medium heat for 15 minutes, shaking the saucepan from time to time.
- Discard any mussels that are still shut.
- Serve immediately while the mussels are still hot, with plenty of bread to soak up the juice.

Prawn Patia

This is an old favourite and one of the very few sweet and sour dishes in Indian cuisine. Many restaurants add mango chutney and tomato sauce to get the sweet and sour flavour.

The method below shows a more authentic technique.

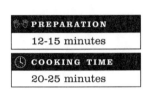

PREPARATION
12-15 minutes

COOKING TIME
20-25 minutes

INGREDIENTS

4 tbsp of cooking oil

2 medium sized onions, finely chopped

3 tomatoes, chopped

1/2 tsp salt

1/2 tsp red chilli powder

1/2 tsp ginger pulp

1/2 tsp garlic pulp

500g (1lb) fresh peeled prawns

2 sprigs of fresh coriander, finely chopped

Sweet and sour tamarind sauce:

2 tsp tamarind paste

1 tbsp tomato paste

1 tsp red chilli powder

1 tsp ginger pulp

1 tsp garlic pulp

1 tsp salt

1 tsp ground coriander

1 tsp white sugar

300ml (10fl oz) warm water

METHOD

• In a bowl, mix together all the ingredients for the sweet and sour tamarind sauce and set aside.

• Heat the oil in a saucepan over a medium heat, add the onion and fry until brown.

• Lower the heat and add the tomatoes, red chilli powder, salt, ginger and garlic and fry for a further 2 minutes.

• Gently add the prawns and stir-fry for 5 minutes. (Be careful not to stir the prawns too aggressively or some may break.)

• Pour in the tamarind sauce and cook, stirring over a medium heat for 10 minutes or until the sauce has thickened.

• Stir in the freshly chopped coriander and serve with boiled rice or bread of your choice.

Prawns with Chickpeas

This recipe is a tasty combination of chickpeas and prawns. We normally used canned chickpeas when preparing this dish to save time but you can, if you wish, soak dried chickpeas overnight ready for use. There's nothing too complicated about this dish, so you shouldn't have any trouble with it.

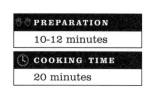

PREPARATION
10-12 minutes

COOKING TIME
20 minutes

INGREDIENTS

4 tbsp of cooking oil

2 bay leaves

$1/2$ tsp onion seeds

2 medium sized onions, finely chopped

1 tsp ginger pulp

1 tsp garlic pulp

1 tsp red chilli powder

$1/2$ tsp turmeric powder

1 tsp salt

2 tbsp lemon juice

500g (1lb) fresh peeled prawns

1 x 425g (14oz) can chickpeas, drained

60ml (2fl oz) warm water

2 sprigs of fresh coriander, finely chopped

METHOD

• Heat the oil over a medium heat in a large saucepan and fry the bay leaves, onion seeds and finely chopped onions for 5 minutes.

• Lower the heat and add the ginger, garlic, red chilli powder, turmeric powder, salt and lemon juice and mix together for around 2 minutes.

• Increase the heat to medium, carefully add the prawns and stir-fry for around 5 minutes.

• Add the chickpeas and cook for 2-3, minutes stirring not more than twice.

• Stir in the warm water cover and simmer for 5 minutes. Stir in the freshly chopped coriander and serve with chapatis (see p80).

7. SIDE DISHES

Tarka Dhaal

This dish is found on the menus of most Indian restaurants worldwide, although the quality varies from restaurant to restaurant.

Some people make this really hot but it's probably best prepared as a side dish with a contrast in potency to the other main dishes. Dhaal (lentils) are a good source of protein.

PREPARATION
10 minutes

COOKING TIME
40 minutes

INGREDIENTS

175g (6oz) Masoor dhaal (red split lentils)

500ml (20fl oz) warm water

$\frac{1}{2}$ tsp turmeric powder

$\frac{1}{2}$ tsp red chilli powder

1 tsp salt

1 fresh green chilli, chopped

3 tbsp of oil

1 medium sized onion, chopped

1 tbsp ginger pulp

1 tbsp garlic pulp

$\frac{1}{2}$ tsp cumin seeds

4 cloves

1 tomato finely chopped

1 sprig of fresh coriander leaves, finely chopped

METHOD

- Wash the dhaal thoroughly, drain, and put in a pan.
- Add the warm water, turmeric powder, red chilli powder and salt and cook on a medium heat, partially covered, for 10-12 minutes.
- Remove the lid and add the freshly chopped green chilli. Now cover the pan and simmer for 20 minutes stirring occasionally.
- Remove the dhaal from the heat and mash.
- Heat the oil in a saucepan, add the onion, ginger, garlic, cumin seeds and cloves and fry for about 3-4 minutes.
- Add the tomato and half of the freshly chopped coriander and stir for about 2 minutes.
- Add half the fried onion mixture to the dhaal, stir in, and turn the dhaal into a serving dish. Pour the remaining fried onion mixture on top, and garnish with the remaining fresh coriander on top.
- Serve with bay fried rice (p84) and puris (p81).

Turnip Curry
(Selgum)

Turnips are normally found in the wetter parts of India. The secret to cooking turnip properly is to do it slowly so that they become tender but don't disintegrate.

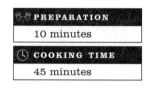

PREPARATION
10 minutes

COOKING TIME
45 minutes

INGREDIENTS

750g (1.5lb) small, sweet turnips

60ml (2fl oz) cooking oil

1 large onion, finely chopped

1 tsp red chilli powder

1 tsp turmeric powder

1 tsp ground cumin

1 tsp ground coriander

1 tsp poppy seeds

2 tsp sesame seeds

1 tsp garlic pulp

2 tsp ginger pulp

1 tsp salt

300ml (10fl oz) warm water

300ml (10fl oz) unsweetened, plain natural yoghurt

1 sprig of fresh coriander leaves, finely chopped

METHOD

- Peel the turnips and cut into slices about 1cm (½-inch) thick.
- Heat the oil in a saucepan and fry the turnips until they begin to change colour.
- Lift them out with a slotted spoon and put to one side.
- Fry the onion in the remaining oil and then add the chilli powder, turmeric, cumin, coriander, poppy and sesame seeds, ginger and garlic and continue to cook for 5-6 minutes.
- Add the warm water, bring to the boil and then add the salt and turnips.
- Continue to boil for 20 minutes and then gently stir in the yoghurt.
- Cook for a further 10 minutes until the turnips are soft.
- Sprinkle on the fresh coriander and serve with chapatis (see p80).

Undey aur Mattar Ka Salan
(Egg and Peas Curry)

This recipe – quite a light one – is fairly dry and is best served with the bread of your choice. It can also be used as a starter.

A good winter warmer after coming off a wet hill in the Highlands.

PREPARATION
15 minutes

COOKING TIME
35 minutes

INGREDIENTS

4 tbsp of oil

1 large onion, chopped

1 tsp cumin seeds

1 x 2.5 cm (1-inch) cinnamon stick

1 tsp ginger pulp

1 tsp garlic pulp

1 tsp tomato paste

1 tomato finely chopped

1 tsp salt

1 tsp red chilli powder

½ tsp turmeric powder

225g (8oz) frozen garden peas (thawed)

125 ml (4fl oz) warm water

13 hard-boiled eggs, shelled

½ tsp garam masala

1 sprig of fresh coriander leaves, finely chopped

METHOD

- Heat the oil in a saucepan and add the finely chopped onion. Fry until soft, then stir in the cumin seeds and cinnamon stick and fry for 3-4 minutes. Add the ginger, garlic, tomato paste and the quartered tomatoes and continue frying gently for 1 minute.
- Add the salt, red chilli powder and turmeric powder and the thawed peas and fry until the mixture is fairly thick.
- Stir in the warm water and carefully add the eggs, cover the saucepan with a lid and simmer gently for 10-15 minutes, stirring the edges of the saucepan occasionally. This will stop the eggs breaking up.
- Once the dish is ready sprinkle on the garam masala and garnish with chopped coriander.
- If preferred, remove the cinnamon stick before serving.

Aloo Palak
(Dry Potato and Spinach)

This potato and spinach curry can be served as a main dish or can be enjoyed as a side dish. On occasion we have used this as a toastie filling.

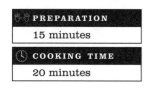

PREPARATION
15 minutes

COOKING TIME
20 minutes

INGREDIENTS

225g (8oz) potatoes, peeled and cut into chunks

50g (2oz) melted, unsalted butter (1)

2 tsp ginger pulp

2 tsp garlic pulp

2 green chillies, finely chopped

½ tsp turmeric powder

1 tsp salt

2 sprigs of fresh coriander leaves, finely chopped

425g (14 oz) canned spinach, drained

or fresh spinach washed and chopped

30ml (1fl oz) warm water

25g (1oz) melted, unsalted butter (2)

METHOD

- Parboil the potatoes for 5 minutes, drain and set aside.
- Heat the butter (1) over a low to medium heat in a saucepan and fry the potatoes for 2-3 minutes.
- Add the garlic, ginger and the green chillies and fry for 3-4 minutes.
- Stir in the turmeric, salt, freshly chopped coriander and canned or chopped fresh spinach.
- Add the water and continue frying for 12-15 minutes or until the potatoes are tender and the spinach is dry.
- Serve with the melted butter (2) poured onto the top and with cucumber and mint raita (p 23) and chapatis (p80).

8. BARBECUE OR GRILL

Seafood Kebabs with Curried Honey Glaze

PREPARATION

20 minutes
(refrigerate until
ready to cook)

COOKING TIME

10 minutes

INGREDIENTS

500g (1lb) thick fish fillets

250g (8oz) scallops

500g (1 lb) king prawns

1 green pepper

1 red pepper

8 button mushrooms

Curried honey glaze:

50g (2oz) unsalted butter

1 tsp curry powder

2 tsp light soy sauce

$\frac{1}{4}$ tsp turmeric powder

$\frac{1}{4}$ tsp coriander powder

50g (2oz) honey

NOTE: Wooden skewers are the best type of skewers to use for kebabs. You can use metal skewers if you like, but allow them to cool before threading the next batch onto them.

METHOD

- Cut the fish into cubes, trim the scallops, peel and de-vein the prawns, leaving the tails intact. De-seed, core and chop the peppers, and slice the mushrooms.
- Thread the scallops, fish, prawns, peppers and mushrooms onto skewers.
- To make the curried honey glaze: put all the ingredients together in a saucepan and cook at a medium heat until the butter is melted.
- Brush the hot glaze all over the kebabs, cover and refrigerate until ready to cook. Cook over a barbecue or under a grill, turning the kebabs regularly to ensure even cooking throughout.
- Serve with Curried French Dip (see p26), a mixed green salad and bread of your choice.

Lamb Tikka Kebab

In our native city of Glasgow, the famous Sauchiehall Street runs from west to east along the heart of the Victorian city. By day it is busy and bustling, but by night it takes on a movie-set image with tourists, club-goers and locals looking for a good time. Drink and food are a big part of this, and one of the best-loved snacks for clubbers and pubbers is the lamb tikka kebab.

On many occasions we have prepared this snack for both indoor and outdoor eating as it is easy and barbecues well. In summer it can be served with a fresh salad and pitta or chapati along with a cool mint and yoghurt dip. I would highly recommend that preparations for this dish are carried out the day before cooking, although it will marinade in the refrigerator for up to 5 or 6 days.

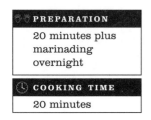

PREPARATION

20 minutes plus
marinading
overnight

COOKING TIME

20 minutes

INGREDIENTS

(Serves 10)

1.5kg (3lb) lamb fillet

1 lemon

450g (³/₄ pint) natural yoghurt

1 tsp salt

1 tsp chilli powder

1 tsp fenugreek leaves

2 tsp tikka paste

2 tsp tandoori paste

1 tsp ginger pulp

2 tsp garlic pulp

1 tsp mint sauce

4 tsp olive oil

1 tsp mango chutney (optional)

¹/₄ tsp red food colour

METHOD

- Cut the lamb into 2.5cm (1-inch) cubes, being careful to remove any fat.
- Cut the lemon in half and squeeze the juice over the lamb.
- In a large bowl or dish add the rest of the ingredients one at a time to the lamb, mixing after each addition. Make sure the lamb is well coated.
- Cover with cling film and refrigerate overnight.
- After taking the bowl out of the fridge, stir the marinaded ingredients thoroughly and begin to push the pieces of lamb on to the skewers.
- Cook each skewer of lamb slowly over a barbecue or under a grill, but be careful not to allow it to cook too quickly on the outside, as it will leave the inside raw. Turn regularly until cooked.

Chicken Tikka Kebab

Another popular carry-out product of the kebab shops. This used to be served as chicken on its own with a few spices sprinkled onto it before being cooked on the gas stove.

Now the chicken is prepared in a tandoori oven and marinaded overnight. Here's how.

PREPARATION

25 minutes plus marinading overnight

COOKING TIME

15-18 minutes

INGREDIENTS

1.3kg (3lb) chicken breasts, cubed

1 lemon

250ml (8fl oz) plain unsweetened yoghurt

1 tsp salt

1 tsp red chilli powder

2 tsp tikka paste

1 tsp tandoori paste

1 tsp ginger pulp

2 tsp garlic pulp

1 tsp mint sauce

4 tbsp of oil

1/4 tsp yellow/orange food colour

NOTE: Wooden skewers are the best type of skewers to use for kebabs. You can use metal skewers if you like, but allow them to cool before threading the next batch on.

METHOD

- Place the cubed chicken breasts in a large bowl. Cut the lemon in half and squeeze the juice over the chicken.
- In a large bowl or dish add the rest of ingredients one at a time to the chicken, mixing after each addition. Make sure that the chicken is well coated.
- Cover with cling film and refrigerate overnight. After taking the bowl out of the fridge, stir the marinaded ingredients thoroughly and begin to push the pieces of chicken onto the skewers.
- Cook each skewer over a barbecue or under a grill, being careful not to allow it to cook too quickly on the outside as this will leave the inside raw. Turn regularly.
- Serve with spiced onions (see p22), Tarka Dhaal (see p49) and bread of your choice.

Tandoori Chicken for Four

If you're having a few people round for dinner, this dish will go down extremely well. This is usually, although inexplicably, very expensive in restaurants.

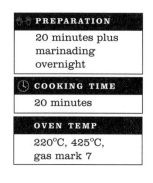

PREPARATION
20 minutes plus marinading overnight

COOKING TIME
20 minutes

OVEN TEMP
220°C, 425°C, gas mark 7

INGREDIENTS

1.3 kg (3lbs) chicken legs or breasts or a combination of the two

1 lemon

250 ml (8oz) plain unsweetened natural yoghurt

1 tsp salt

1 tsp red chilli powder

1 tsp fenugreek leaves

2 tbsp tandoori paste

1 tsp ginger pulp

1 tsp garlic pulp

3 tbsp of oil

1/4 tsp of red food colouring

1 sprig of fresh coriander leaves, finely chopped

1 tsp tomato paste

NOTE: Wooden skewers are the best type of skewers to use for kebabs. You can use metal skewers if you like, but allow them to cool before threading the next batch on.

METHOD

• Remove skin from the chicken and cut each piece in half. With a sharp knife make regular slits through the chicken portions.

• Cut the lemon in half and squeeze the juice over the chicken, then rub in the salt.

• In a large bowl or dish add the rest of ingredients one at a time to the chicken, mixing after each addition. Make sure that the pieces, especially the slits, are well coated.

• Cover with cling film and refrigerate overnight.

• After taking the bowl out of the fridge, stir the marinaded ingredients thoroughly and begin to push 2 pieces of chicken on each skewer.

• Cook each skewer of chicken slowly over a barbecue or under a grill, being careful not to allow it to cook too quickly on the outside as this will leave the inside raw. Turn regularly.

• Serve with lemon and lime wedges.

9. HEALTHY OPTIONS

King Prawn and Mango Salad with Coconut Dressing

King prawns have next to no fat on them so this is an ideal dish for the weight watcher

PREPARATION
10 minutes

COOKING TIME
15-17 minutes

INGREDIENTS

750g (1.5lb) cooked king prawns

1 crispy lettuce

2 mangoes, peeled, stoned and chopped

1 tomato, chopped

Coconut dressing:

2 tsp sugar

2 tbsp lemon juice

$\frac{1}{2}$ tsp curry powder

$\frac{1}{4}$ tsp turmeric powder

1 tbsp grated fresh ginger

125ml (4fl oz) coconut cream

METHOD

- Shell and de-vein the prawns leaving the tails intact.
- Wash the lettuce under cold water and place the leaves onto serving plates, top with the prawns, mangoes and chopped tomato, then the dressing (see below).
- For the coconut dressing, place all the ingredients in a jar and shake well.

Red Salmon and Basil Salad

This dish is a healthy accompaniment to barbecue foods and can be included as part of a platter or on its own as a starter.

PREPARATION
10 minutes

INGREDIENTS

440g (15 oz) fresh red salmon, cut into 1-inch pieces

3 tbsp lemon juice

200g (7oz) cherry tomatoes, halved

4 radishes, sliced

2 tbsp fresh basil leaves

2 sprigs fresh mint leaves

1 crispy lettuce

Dressing:

2 garlic cloves crushed

1 tbsp lemon juice

$1/4$ tsp garam masala

$1/4$ tsp red chilli powder (optional)

30ml (1fl oz) olive oil

- Remove the skin and bones from the salmon.
- Place the salmon in a bowl, add the lemon juice, tomatoes, radishes, mint leaves, and basil, then mix in the dressing (see below).
- Wash the lettuce under cold water, and place the leaves onto serving plates, top with the salmon mixture.
- For the dressing, combine all the ingredients in a jar and shake well.

Chicken and Pineapple Salad with Curried Mayonnaise

A new recipe but one we're sure you'll enjoy. This is another summer dish, and is ideal when you've overdone it the night before and want something light to get the taste buds going again. A fine blend of sweet and savoury.

PREPARATION

10 minutes plus
1 hour for
rerigeration

INGREDIENTS

50g (2oz) shredded coconut

1 barbecued chicken

3 green shallots, chopped

400g (14oz) unsweetened pineapple chunks, drained

Curried mayonnaise:

1 clove garlic crushed

$1/2$ tsp curry powder

$1/2$ tsp red chilli powder

$1/4$ tsp turmeric powder

60 ml (2fl oz) coconut milk

100g (4oz) mayonnaise

METHOD

• Toast the coconut in the oven on a moderate heat for 5-7 minutes. Strip and cut the chicken into chunks, and place in a large bowl.

• For the curried mayonnaise, place all the ingredients in a bowl and mix thoroughly.

• Mix in the pineapple, coconut, shallots and chicken and refrigerate for 1 hour before serving.

Chilli Chicken Salad

The combination of the spice with chicken coupled with the soy sauce provides an interesting zesty contrast in flavours. Again, this is highly recommended for summer, although good all year round, and easy to make. Note: this recipe uses raw egg.

PREPARATION
10 minutes plus 1 hour for refrigeration

COOKING TIME
20-25 minutes

INGREDIENTS

2 tbsp sesame seeds

200g (7oz) snow peas

4 chicken breast fillets, skinned

1 tsp cornflour

1 tbsp sweet soy sauce

1 tbsp olive oil

200g (7oz) can of butterbeans, drained

4 green shallots chopped

2-3 green chillies chopped

1 sprig of fresh coriander, finely chopped

1 tbsp whisky (optional)

For the dressing:
75ml (3fl oz) olive oil

1 tbsp lemon juice

1 tbsp light soy sauce

$1/2$ tsp garam masala

$1/2$ tsp red chilli powder

1 tsp grated fresh ginger

1 tsp sugar

1 egg yolk

METHOD

- Toast the sesame seeds by stirring in a saucepan over a medium heat. Allow to cool.
- Top and tail the snow peas and boil them in water for 2-3 minutes. Drain immediately, then rinse them under cold water until they are cold.
- Cut the chicken into thin strips and place in a bowl. Add the cornflour and sweet soy sauce and mix well.
- Heat the oil in a large saucepan or wok, and stir-fry the chicken in batches over a medium to high heat until tender and light brown all over. Remove from the pan or wok and cool.
- Combine the chicken, sesame seeds, butter beans, shallots, green chillies and coriander in a large bowl. Stir in the dressing (see below) and refrigerate for 1 hour. Add the snow peas before serving.
- For the dressing, combine all the ingredients in a jar and shake well.

9. STIR-FRY

Stir-fried Chicken

This chicken dish is beautifully aromatic and can be made in the wok or in a deep frying pan. When stir-frying ensure the chicken is cut into similar sized pieces so that they can cook evenly.

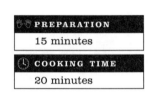

PREPARATION
15 minutes

COOKING TIME
20 minutes

INGREDIENTS

4 tbsp of oil

2 medium sized onions, chopped

2 bay leaves

1 tbsp Indian medium curry paste

1/2 tsp red chilli powder

1/4 tsp turmeric powder

1/2 tsp ground cumin

1/2 tsp ginger pulp

1 tsp garlic pulp

500g (1lb) boneless chicken breast cut into small pieces

1 tsp salt

1 green pepper, cored, deseeded and chopped

14 button mushrooms, washed and quartered

1 tsp fenugreek leaves

1 sprig of fresh coriander leaves, finely chopped

METHOD

• Heat the oil in a wok or deep pan and fry the onions and bay leaves over a medium heat for about 3 minutes.

• Add the curry paste, red chilli powder, turmeric powder, ground cumin, ginger and garlic and stir-fry for a further minute.

• Remove the wok/deep pan from the heat then add the chicken and salt. Return the pan to a medium heat and stir-fry for around 8-9 minutes.

• Add in the green peppers, mushrooms and fenugreek leaves and stir-fry for a further 4–5 minutes.

• Stir in half the chopped coriander and sprinkle the remaining half on top.

• Serve immediately with boiled rice.

Stir-fried Green Pepper and Baby Corn in Garlic Butter

It is important that you use fresh garlic cloves to prepare this dish as it gives a beautiful aroma. Although we have suggested green pepper and baby corn for this recipe, you can really use any vegetables that you choose.

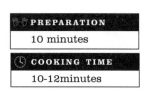

PREPARATION
10 minutes

COOKING TIME
10-12minutes

INGREDIENTS

75g (3oz) unsalted butter

1 tbsp of oil

5 garlic cloves, peeled and crushed

1 tsp onion seeds

1 red chilli, finely chopped

1 sprig of fresh mint, chopped

1 sprig of fresh coriander, chopped

1 tsp salt

1 tsp brown sugar

1 tsp lemon juice

8-10 shallots, chopped

300g (8oz) baby corn

1 green pepper, cored and thickly sliced

1 tsp black pepper

METHOD

- Heat the butter with the oil in a wok and fry the garlic, onion seeds and chopped red chilli for 2 minutes.
- In a bowl mix together the fresh mint, fresh coriander, salt, brown sugar and lemon juice, and add to the wok with the shallots, baby corn and green pepper.
- Stir-fry for around 8 minutes over a medium heat. Sprinkle with the black pepper and serve.
- Serve with boiled rice.

Stir-fried King Prawns

This, too, is very straightforward and can made with the minimum of fuss. It can be made in quantities for one person or six people in roughly the same time, just remember to adjust the amount of spice for the numbers being served.

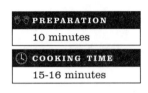

PREPARATION
10 minutes

COOKING TIME
15-16 minutes

INGREDIENTS

1 tsp garlic pulp

1 tsp ginger pulp

1 tsp coriander powder

$1/2$ tsp red chilli powder

4 tbsp of water

16 raw king prawns in shells

4 tbsp of oil

$1/2$ tsp onion seeds

3 bay leaves

4 spring onions, trimmed and roughly chopped

1 tsp salt

1 tomato, diced

4 fresh mint leaves, finely chopped

2 sprigs of coriander leaves, finely chopped

1 tbsp lemon juice

Lime wedges to garnish (optional)

METHOD

- In a bowl mix together the garlic, ginger, coriander powder, red chilli powder and water, and mix to a paste. Blend the spice mixture into the king prawns and set aside.
- Heat the oil in a wok and stir-fry the onion seeds and bay leaves for 1 minute.
- Add the spring onions and stir-fry them for 3-4 minutes until golden brown.
- Add the prawn mixture and salt, and stir-fry for around 5 minutes, reduce the heat if necessary. Add the diced tomato, chopped mint and chopped coriander.
- Sprinkle in the lemon juice and gently stir-fry for 5-6 minutes and serve with boiled rice.

Stir-fried Beef with Green Pepper

Another very easy dish to prepare. This only takes minutes once it's been marinaded.

PREPARATION

10 minutes plus 2 hours for marinading

COOKING TIME

17-19 minutes

INGREDIENTS

350g (12oz) beef strips for stir-fry

1 tsp garlic pulp

1/2 tsp garam masala

1 tbsp light soy sauce

1 tsp salt

1 tsp ground black pepper

125g (4oz) basmati rice (cook the rice according to the packet instructions. Drain, rinse with cold water and set aside)

3 tbsp of oil

3 bay leaves

1 green pepper, deseeded and cut into strips

50g (2oz) bean sprouts, washed

4 spring onions, trimmed and roughly chopped

2 sprigs of fresh coriander, finely chopped

METHOD

- In a large bowl, mix together the beef, garlic, garam masala, soy sauce, salt and black pepper. Cover and leave to marinade for 2 hours.
- Meanwhile, cook the rice.
- Heat the oil in a wok. Add the beef mixture and bay leaves and stir-fry for 8-10 minutes, reduce the heat if necessary. Add the green pepper to the wok and stir-fry for 3 minutes.
- Add the cooked rice and the green peppers to the beef mixture, and stir-fry for 3 minutes.
- Stir in the bean sprouts, spring onions and freshly chopped coriander. Stir-fry for 1 minute and serve.

10. PDQ (PRETTY DAMN QUICK!) DISHES

Indian Toast

This is a popular breakfast dish for many Indian families and is delicious when freshly cooked, although it can be kept and eaten as a snack – hot or cold – later on the same day.

PREPARATION
5 minutes

COOKING TIME
4-5 minutes per slice of bread

INGREDIENTS

1 green chilli, finely chopped

$1/2$ tsp red chilli powder

$1/4$ tsp black pepper

$1/4$ tsp turmeric powder

$1/4$ tsp salt

1 sprig of fresh coriander, finely chopped

4 eggs

Oil for shallow frying

4 slices of plain or brown bread

METHOD

- In a large bowl, combine the green chilli, red chilli powder, black pepper, turmeric powder, salt and chopped coriander.
- Add the eggs and mix well.
- Heat a little (3 tbsp) of oil over a low to medium heat in a large frying pan.
- Soak both sides of the bread in the egg mixture and shallow fry on each side for 2-3 minutes.
- Repeat with the remaining bread and serve immediately.

Curried Baked Beans

Who'd have thought it! Try making these with fresh ingredients and serve immediately. Good for a quick snack served with bread or on toast and ideal for making on the hills during a climb or walk.

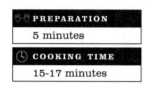

PREPARATION
5 minutes

COOKING TIME
15-17 minutes

INGREDIENTS

3 tbsp of oil

1 small onion, finely chopped

1 tsp ginger pulp

$\frac{1}{2}$ tsp garlic pulp

$\frac{1}{2}$ tsp red chilli powder

$\frac{1}{2}$ tsp coriander powder

$\frac{1}{2}$ tsp turmeric powder

$\frac{1}{2}$ tsp salt

1 tbsp tomato paste

420g (15oz) can of baked beans

60ml (2fl oz) warm water

METHOD

- Heat the oil in a saucepan over a medium heat and fry the onion until brown.
- Add the ginger, garlic, red chilli powder, coriander powder, turmeric powder, tomato paste and salt and stir-fry for 2 minutes.
- Add the beans, stir in the warm water and cover the saucepan with a lid. Simmer for 8-10 minutes and serve with the bread of your choice.

Spicy Egg Curry with Mushroom and Tomato

We often have this curry on sandwiches and it makes a very filling and tasty snack. It's not vegan but is generally acceptable for vegetarians.

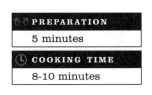

PREPARATION
5 minutes

COOKING TIME
8-10 minutes

INGREDIENTS

4 tbsp of oil

1 medium sized onion, finely chopped

2 green chillies, finely chopped

1 tsp garlic pulp

1 tsp ginger pulp

125g (5oz) button mushrooms, chopped

1 tomato, chopped

5 eggs

1 tsp salt

1 tsp black pepper

1 tsp red chilli powder

$\frac{1}{2}$ tsp turmeric powder

1 sprig of fresh coriander leaves, finely chopped

METHOD

- Heat the oil on a low to medium heat in a large saucepan and fry the onion until soft.
- Add the green chillies, garlic and ginger and stir for 1 minute.
- Add the mushrooms and tomato and stir-fry for a further 2 minutes.
- In a bowl, beat the eggs together with the salt, black pepper, red chilli powder and turmeric and then add the coriander leaves.
- Pour the mixture into the saucepan and mix in well, lower the heat slightly and continue to cook as scrambled, remembering to scrape the sides and bottom of the saucepan whilst cooking.
- Once the eggs are cooked they are ready to serve. Serve with chapatis (see p80).

Spicy Chicken and Chips

A quick dish that we cook all the time for friends and family.

PREPARATION
5-7 minutes

COOKING TIME
20 minutes

INGREDIENTS

2 tbsp of oil

1 shallot, roughly chopped

1 tbsp tomato paste

$1/4$ tsp garlic pulp

$1/4$ tsp ginger pulp

$1/4$ tsp red chilli powder

$1/4$ tsp turmeric powder

1 green chilli, finely chopped

$1/4$ tsp salt

2 cloves

1 chicken breast, skinned and cubed into bite sized pieces

60 ml (2fl oz) warm water

1 small sprig of fresh coriander leaves, finely chopped

$1/4$ tsp fenugreek leaves

METHOD

- Heat the oil in a frying pan and fry the shallot over a medium heat until soft.
- Add the tomato paste, garlic, ginger, red chilli powder, turmeric powder, green chilli, salt and cloves and stir-fry for 2 minutes.
- Add the chicken cubes and stir-fry for 3 minutes.
- Add the water, stir in the fenugreek leaves, cover the frying pan with a lid and simmer for 10 minutes, checking and stirring no more than twice.
- Stir in the fresh coriander, stir-fry for 2 minutes and serve over hot chips.

11. Oven Dishes

Butter chicken

This recipe has been a true favourite in Indian restaurants worldwide. There are several versions, although this is one of our favourites and is very easy to prepare.

PREPARATION
20 minutes plus 5-6 hours for marinading

COOKING TIME
50 minutes

OVEN TEMP
220°C, 425°C, gas mark 7

INGREDIENTS

1.5kg (3-3.5lb) chicken, skinned and cut into 8 pieces

1 lemon

$\frac{1}{2}$ tsp salt

$\frac{1}{2}$ tsp ginger pulp

1 tsp garlic pulp

$\frac{1}{2}$ tsp red chilli powder

1 tsp tomato paste

$\frac{1}{4}$ tsp turmeric powder

$\frac{1}{2}$ tsp coriander powder

$\frac{1}{4}$ tsp orange food colouring (optional)

For the sauce:

100g (4oz) unsalted butter

150g (5oz) plain, unsweetened yoghurt

125ml (4oz) soured cream

METHOD

- With a sharp knife make regular slits through the chicken portions and place in a large bowl.
- Cut the lemon in half, squeeze the juice over the chicken and rub in the salt. Mix in the ginger, garlic, red chilli powder, tomato paste, turmeric powder, coriander powder and the orange food colouring, cover and set aside for 5-6 hours to marinade in the fridge.
- Place the chicken portions in a greased baking tray and cook in a preheated oven for 50 minutes, brushing occasionally with a little melted butter.
- Melt the unsalted butter in a saucepan, add the remaining marinade and the soured cream. Gently heat at a low temperature for 3-4 minutes.
- Pour the sauce over the baked chicken and serve with a mixed green salad, rice and bread of your choice.

Seekh Kebabs

These kebabs are highly aromatic and can be eaten on their own or as an accompaniment with a main course. When you are buying the mince ask for it to be run through the mincer twice to make it finer. These kebabs are also delicious barbecued.

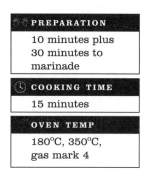

PREPARATION
10 minutes plus
30 minutes to
marinade

COOKING TIME
15 minutes

OVEN TEMP
180°C, 350°C,
gas mark 4

INGREDIENTS

1 small sized onion, finely chopped

1 green chilli seeded, and finely chopped

1 sprig of fresh coriander leaves, finely chopped

2 cloves

Juice of half a lemon

500g (1lb) lean mince beef or lamb

1 egg yolk

1/4 tsp red chilli powder

1 tsp salt

1/2 tsp ground cumin

1/2 tsp ground ajwain

1/2 tsp garam masala

1 tsp ginger pulp

1 tsp garlic pulp

2 tbsp of oil

Wooden skewers are the best type to use for kebabs. You can use metal skewers if you like, but allow them to cool before threading the next batch onto them.

METHOD

• In a liquidiser or blender, grind the onion, green chilli, coriander, mint, cloves and lemon juice to a smooth paste. Transfer the mixture to a large bowl.

• Add the meat to the liquidised paste in the bowl.

• Add the rest of the ingredients, except the oil and knead the mixture until all the ingredients are mixed thoroughly.

• Set aside for 10-15 minutes – this will allow the egg to bind the mixture together.

• Shape some of the meat mixture around the skewer to a length of about 10cm (4 inches) and place on a roasting tray. Make the rest of the kebabs the same way.

• Brush the kebabs with a little oil and place the roasting tray under a preheated grill (180 °C-350°F), cook for 6-7 minutes on each side.

• Remove the tray from the grill, brush the remaining oil onto the kebabs and grill for around 7-8 minutes, turning the kebabs regularly to ensure even cooking throughout.

• Serve with lemon wedges, mint chutney (p24) and bread of your choice.

Spicy Fish Fillets

A light dish and easy to prepare, this can be ready in about 25 minutes.

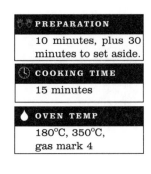

PREPARATION
10 minutes, plus 30 minutes to set aside.

COOKING TIME
15 minutes

OVEN TEMP
180°C, 350°C, gas mark 4

INGREDIENTS

4x 175g (4x 6oz) white fish fillets

1 tsp red chilli powder

1 tsp garam masala

1 tsp lemon juice

1/2 tsp ground black pepper

1/2 tsp ginger pulp

1/2 tsp garlic pulp

1/2 tsp coriander powder

METHOD

- Mix the spices, salt, pepper and lemon juice in a bowl.
- Rub this mixture well into the fish and set aside for 30 minutes.
- Place in a preheated oven for 15 minutes, gently turning once, halfway through.
- Serve with lemon and lime wedges.

Dum Ka Raan
(Roast Leg of Lamb)

This takes a few hours to prepare so make sure all the right spices are in place, and give yourself plenty of preparation time.

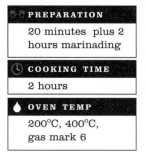

PREPARATION	20 minutes plus 2 hours marinading
COOKING TIME	2 hours
OVEN TEMP	200°C, 400°C, gas mark 6

INGREDIENTS

2kg (4.4lb) lean leg of lamb

2 tbsp ginger pulp

2 tbsp garlic pulp

2 tbsp lemon juice

1 tsp salt

1 tsp ground coriander

1 tsp red chilli powder

1 tsp cumin powder

1 tsp garam masala

2 sprigs fresh mint

1 tbsp tomato paste

100g (4oz) plain, unsweetened yoghurt

5 tbsp of oil

METHOD

- In a large bowl mix the ginger, garlic, lemon juice, salt, ground spices, mint, tomato paste, yoghurt and oil.
- Make 4-5 2.5cm (1-inch) deep cuts across the leg of lamb.
- Rub in the spice mixture, cover and refrigerate for around 2 hours.
- Cook in a pre-heated oven for 25 minutes to seal the juices, then cover the leg of lamb with tin foil and continue cooking for 1hour and 35 minutes or until the meat is tender.
- Serve with cucumber and mint raita (p23), spiced onions (p22), matter pilau (p83) and bread of your choice.

12. Dishes Containing Alcohol

Prawns with Pernod and Almonds

Be careful that you don't overdo the Pernod in this or you won't be able to taste anything else. This is another of our inventions.

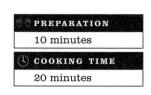

PREPARATION
10 minutes

COOKING TIME
20 minutes

INGREDIENTS

500g(1lb) fresh peeled prawns

25g(1oz) unsalted butter

1 medium sized onion, finely chopped

2 garlic cloves, crushed

$^1/_4$ tsp salt

$^1/_4$ tsp garam masala

2 x 400g (2 x 14oz) chopped, canned tomatoes

60ml (2fl oz) Pernod

25g (1oz) ground almonds

50g (2oz) double cream

$^1/_2$ tsp black pepper

METHOD

• Peel and de-vein the prawns leaving the tails intact.
• Heat the butter in a saucepan, add the chopped onion and fry until soft.
• Add the crushed garlic, salt and garam masala and cook for 1 minute, then add the tomatoes and Pernod and bring to the boil.
• Reduce the heat and simmer uncovered for 10 minutes.
• Add the prawns, ground almonds and cream, cook for about 5 minutes or until the prawns change colour, stir in the black pepper and serve immediately.
• Serve with matter pilau (p83) and puris (p81).

Mumbai Fish Curry

Mumbai, formerly known as Bombay, is a place we've been to many times, visiting family, and experiencing new cooking techniques.

It is a place that never ceases to amaze, and the hustle and bustle of the street food vendors and other eateries adds to the excitement.

We have produced some delicious recipes by mixing our own cooking styles with those we've come across in Mumbai. Never be afraid to adapt a recipe to your own taste.

PREPARATION
10 minutes

COOKING TIME
25 minutes

INGREDIENTS

60ml (2fl oz) cooking oil

1 medium sized onion, finely chopped

2 red chillies, very finely chopped

1 tsp garlic pulp

1 tsp ginger pulp

1 tsp ground turmeric

1 tsp ground coriander

$\frac{1}{2}$ tsp black pepper

50g (2oz) desiccated coconut

1 tsp salt

$\frac{1}{2}$ glass of medium to dry white wine

1 sprig of fresh parsley, finely chopped

1kg (2.2lb) fillets of white fish, cut into 2.5 cm (1-inch) pieces

1 lemon

METHOD

- Heat the oil in a saucepan and fry the onion until soft.
- Add the red chillies, garlic, ginger, turmeric powder, coriander powder and black pepper. Stir-fry for 2 minutes.
- Add the warm water and coconut. Add the salt and bring to the boil, then add the white wine and parsley. Continue to boil for 1 minute.
- Add the fish pieces and simmer for 15 minutes until the fish is cooked.
- Squeeze in the lemon juice and serve with boiled rice and chapatis (p80).

Special Chicken and Prawn Delight

Warning! This dish will seriously hit your taste buds and enhance your thoughts on Indian cuisine. Use cooking whisky if you are religious about malts.

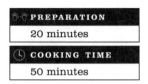

PREPARATION
20 minutes

COOKING TIME
50 minutes

INGREDIENTS

5 tbsp of oil

1 tsp cumin seeds

2 medium sized onions, finely chopped

500g (1lb) chicken breast, cubed

1 tsp garlic pulp

1 tsp ginger pulp

1 tomato, skinned and diced

1/2 tsp turmeric powder

1/2 tsp red chilli powder

2 tbsp tomato paste

1/2 tsp ajwain

1 tsp tandoori paste

125ml (4fl oz) warm water

300g (10oz) fresh peeled prawns

1 tsp salt

1 tsp ground cashew nuts

175ml (6fl oz) single cream

25ml (1fl oz) whisky,
any malt of your choice

1 tsp garam masala

To garnish:

1 pineapple ring

1 red cherry

25g (1oz) flaked almonds

1 sprig of freshly chopped
coriander, finely chopped

METHOD

- Heat the oil over a medium heat in a large saucepan and fry the cumin seeds until they begin to crackle. Add the onions and fry them until light brown.
- Add the chicken, garlic, ginger and diced tomato and stir-fry for around 5 minutes.
- Stir in the turmeric powder, red chilli powder, tomato paste, ajwain and tandoori paste. Stir-fry for around 2 minutes.
- Gradually stir in the warm water and simmer for 10 minutes. Turn the heat up to medium, add the prawns, salt and ground cashew nuts and simmer for 10 minutes.
- Turn the heat up to medium and gently stir in the single cream and whisky.
- Cover the saucepan with a lid (leaving a half-inch gap) and simmer for around 20 minutes, checking and stirring occasionally.
- Stir in the garam masala, place in a serving dish and garnish with chopped fresh coriander, pineapple ring, red cherry and almond flakes and serve as main dish.
- Serve with bay fried rice (p84).

13. Hot Curry Selection

Prawn Chilli Masala

This is a richly flavoured dish. Just when you thought it was safe to swallow the mild cool taste, you'll get a good kick from the rich, aromatic chillies.

PREPARATION
15 minutes

COOKING TIME
20 minutes

INGREDIENTS

100g (4oz) unsalted butter

4 green cardamoms, bruised

1/2 tsp turmeric powder

1 tsp coriander powder

1 tsp ginger pulp

4 garlic cloves peeled, and crushed

500g (1lb) fresh peeled prawns

100g (4oz) plain unsweetened yoghurt

60ml (2fl oz) warm water

1 tsp salt

1 tsp sugar

4 green chillies, finely chopped

25g (1oz) ground almonds

1 medium sized onion, finely chopped

1 tsp red chilli powder

1/2 tsp garam masala

1 sprig of fresh coriander,
finely chopped

METHOD

- In a large saucepan melt 50g (2fl oz) butter over a gentle heat and fry the green cardamoms for 1 minute. Add the turmeric powder, ground coriander, ginger, garlic and red chilli powder. Continue to stir and fry for a further minute.

- Add the prawns, and cook for 5 minutes, stirring occasionally. Turn the heat up to medium and stir in the yoghurt. Gradually add the water.

- Stir in the salt and sugar, cover the pan and cook for 5 minutes.

- Add the green chillies and ground almonds and cook uncovered over a low to medium heat for 4-5 minutes.

- Meanwhile, fry the onion in the remaining 50g (2fl oz) of unsalted butter until brown.

- Stir this mixture into the prawns and cook for a further 2 minutes.

- Stir in the garam masala and garnish with the freshly chopped coriander and serve.

- Serve with mint chutney (p24) and chapatis (p80).

Chilli-Spiced Chicken Curry

This is another one that's on the hot side, so be careful if you're having friends round.

PREPARATION
15 minutes

COOKING TIME
50-55 minutes

INGREDIENTS

6 tbsp of cooking oil

6-8 fresh green chillies, slit in the middle

2 medium sized onions, finely chopped

4 bay leaves

2 tsp brown sugar

1 tsp tamarind paste

1/2 tsp red chilli powder

1 tsp garlic pulp

1 tsp ginger pulp

1 tsp ground cumin

1 tsp turmeric powder

1 tsp ground coriander

1 tsp salt

300ml (10fl oz) warm water

1 kg (2.2lb) chicken, skinned and cut into small pieces

1 sprig of fresh coriander, finely chopped

1 sprig of fresh mint, finely chopped

1 tomato, chopped

1 tsp sesame seeds

METHOD

- Heat the oil in a large saucepan over a high heat and fry the chillies for 1 minute. Lower the heat then remove the chillies from the pan with a slotted spoon and set aside.
- Turn the heat up to medium and add the onions and bay leaves. Cook until the onions turn brown.
- While the onions are frying, mix together the brown sugar, tamarind paste, red chilli powder, garlic, ginger, ground cumin, turmeric powder, ground coriander, salt and half the warm water in a small bowl to form a paste.
- Once the onions turn brown lower the heat, and gently pour in the spice mixture. Stir-fry for about 2-3 minutes.
- Add the chicken pieces, then stir in the remaining warm water and cook over a low to medium heat for about 30-35 minutes, checking and stirring 2-3 times.
- Stir in the fresh coriander, fresh mint, tomato and sesame seeds. Cook for a further 5 minutes and serve with boiled rice or bread of your choice.

Lamb Vindaloo

Vindaloo is made by marinading the meat in spices and vinegar. This is a fairly hot dish so watch out. The word 'vindaloo' is often used to describe an incredibly hot dish and it used to be a huge mistake to ask for a vindaloo in a restaurant because chefs would often go over the top with the chilli spice.

'Vindaloo' has nothing to do with vast amounts of chilli in the dish. It is a combination of the Portugese word 'vin' (wine) and the Indian word 'aloo' (potato). The following recipe is much more palatable than the 'traditional' vindaloo.

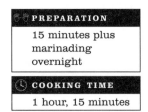

PREPARATION

15 minutes plus
marinading
overnight

COOKING TIME

1 hour, 15 minutes

INGREDIENTS

**Grind the following 3 ingredients
in a blender or coffee grinder:**

6 red chillies

1 tbsp coriander seeds

1 tbsp cumin seeds

1 tsp ginger pulp

2 tsp garlic pulp

1 tsp ground turmeric

1kg (2.2lb) lamb cut into 1-inch cubes

4 tbsp of cooking oil

1 large onion, finely chopped

2 tsp red chilli powder

1 tbsp tomato paste

1 tsp salt

1 tsp garam masala

500ml (20fl oz – 1pint) warm water

1 tsp fenugreek leaves

2 sprigs of fresh coriander, finely chopped

METHOD

- In a large bowl, add the vinegar and freshly ground spices and mix together with a wooden spoon to form a thick paste. Add the ginger, garlic and turmeric powder. Mix thoroughly.
- Add the meat and mix it well, making sure it's coated with the paste.
- Cover the bowl with cling film and leave to marinade in the refrigerator overnight.
- Heat the oil in a large saucepan and fry the onion until soft. Add the red chilli powder, tomato paste, salt and garam masala and stir-fry for around 3-4 minutes.
- Add the warm water and bring to the boil. Add the fenugreek leaves, cover the saucepan with a lid and simmer for 50-55 minutes or until the meat is tender, checking and stirring no more than 2-3 times.
- Stir in half the fresh coriander, sprinkle the rest on top and serve.
- Serve with buckets of water, boiled rice and bread of your choice.

Aloo Madras
(Dry Spicy Hot Potato Curry)

In restaurant spice ratings, the 'Madras' ranked only one place below the 'vindaloo' as the hottest dish available. Again, the name 'madras' has nothing to do with the spice factor but is named after the city of the curry's origin, so it's a bit like the 'Forfar Bridie'.

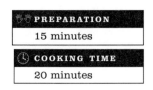

PREPARATION
15 minutes

COOKING TIME
20 minutes

INGREDIENTS

4 tbsp of oil

1 medium sized onion, finely chopped

$\frac{1}{2}$ tsp turmeric powder

1 tsp red chilli powder

$\frac{1}{2}$ tsp salt

1 tsp garlic pulp

4 curry leaves

2 bay leaves

1 tsp tomato paste

500g (1lb) potatoes, half boiled, peeled and cut into chunks

60ml (2fl oz) warm water

2 green chillies, finely chopped

1 tsp fenugreek leaves

METHOD

- Heat the oil in a saucepan and fry the onion until light brown. Stir in the turmeric powder, red chilli powder, salt, garlic pulp, curry leaves, bay leaves, and tomato paste, and stir-fry for 1 minute.
- Add the potatoes and stir in the warm water. Cover the saucepan with a lid and simmer for 5 minutes.
- Lift the lid, add the green chillies and stir in the fenugreek leaves. Cover the saucepan with a lid and continue to simmer for 8-10 minutes, checking and stirring once.
- Serve as a side or main dish with rice or bread of your choice.

14. BREADS

Chapati

Chapatis are cooked almost daily in Indian households. This is one of the less fattening breads.

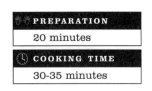

PREPARATION
20 minutes

COOKING TIME
30-35 minutes

INGREDIENTS

250g (8oz) wholemeal or chapati flour,
plus extra for dusting
170ml-280ml (6-10fl oz water)
depending on the texture of the flour
$\frac{1}{2}$ tsp salt

METHOD

- Sift the flour in a large bowl with the salt. Gradually add the water and mix well with your fingers until a pliable dough is formed.
- Knead for about 5 minutes then cover and set aside for 15-20 minutes.
- Divide the dough into about 10-12 balls.
- Hold each ball between your palms and rotate in a circular motion until it is smooth and round, flatten the ball into a round cake and dust lightly with a little chapati flour.
- Roll it out on a well-floured surface to around 15cms (6-inch) diameter.
- Have a tea-towel ready so you can wrap the chapatis up to keep them warm.
- Heat the thawa or a heavy-based frying pan over a medium heat. When it is very hot, lower the heat to medium, place a chapati on the thawa or heavy-based frying pan and after about 30 seconds flip it over.
- Repeat the process for the other side. Press down with a clean tea-towel and turn once again.
- Remove the chapati from the thawa or frying pan and keep warm in a tea-towel. Repeat with the remaining dough.

Puris

(Deep-fried Bread)

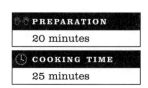

PREPARATION

20 minutes

COOKING TIME

25 minutes

INGREDIENTS

250g (8oz) wholemeal or chapati flour,
plus extra for dusting
170–280ml (6–10fl oz water) quantity
depends on the texture of the flour
$\frac{1}{2}$ tsp salt
Oil for deep frying

METHOD

- Sift the flour in a large bowl with the salt. Gradually add the water and mix well with your fingers until a pliable dough is formed.
- Knead for about 5 minutes, then cover and set aside for 15–20 minutes.
- Divide the dough into about 10–12 balls.
- Hold each ball between your palms and rotate in a circular motion until it is smooth and round.
- Flatten the ball into a round cake and dust lightly with a little chapati flour.
- Roll it out in a well-floured surface to around 15cm (6-inch) diameter.
- Heat 5cm (2-inches) of oil in a deep frying pan and drop a small amount of flour into the oil. If it floats after a couple of seconds the oil is at the correct temperature.
- Slide in 1 puri at a time and fry on both sides until light brown. Lift out the puri with a pair of kitchen tongs and drain on kitchen paper.
- If puris are left uncovered they become crisp. It's best to keep them wrapped in a tea towel or aluminium foil. Repeat with the remaining dough.

15. RICE

Plain Boiled Rice

Plain boiled rice is, of course, extremely versatile. This is probably the easiest recipe in the world. Rice should be washed thoroughly in warm water at least 3-4 times and drained in a sieve.

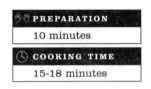

PREPARATION
10 minutes

COOKING TIME
15-18 minutes

INGREDIENTS

275g (10oz) basmati rice

1.5 litre (3pints) water

1/2 tsp salt

METHOD

- Fill a large saucepan with water, add the salt and bring to the boil.
- Gently drop the rice into the saucepan, stir briefly and continue to boil the rice for 12-14 minutes or until the grains are almost cooked. The rice should still have a firm centre.
- Drain the rice and set aside for around 3 minutes. The steam should be enough to cook the centre of each grain.
- Hold sides of the drainer and gently toss the rice – this will help to separate each grain. Stir a fork through the rice before serving.

Matter Pilau

An easy to prepare pilau rice. Peas and rice go very well together and this recipe makes a delicious accompaniment to a good chicken curry.

PREPARATION
10 minutes

COOKING TIME
25 minutes

INGREDIENTS

275g (10oz) basmati rice

50g (2oz) unsalted butter

$1/_2$ tsp cumin seeds

1 tsp fennel seeds

4 cloves

4 green cardamoms, split open each pod

2 bay leaves

1 medium sized onion, finely chopped

1 tsp ground turmeric powder

1 tsp salt

500ml (20fl oz) water

2 cinnamon sticks, 5 cm (2-inches) long

150g (6oz) frozen garden peas

METHOD

- Wash the rice and soak in cold water for 10-15 minutes.
- Melt the butter over a medium heat and stir-fry the cumin and fennel seeds for 2-3 minutes.
- Add the cloves, green cardamoms, bay leaves and onions and continue to fry until the onion turns brown, stirring frequently. Add the turmeric and salt.
- Drain the rice then add to the pan and stir-fry for 1 minute.
- Add the water and bring to the boil. Cover the pan and simmer for 15 minutes without lifting the lid. Remove the pan from the heat and set aside undisturbed for around 10 minutes. Stir a fork through the rice before serving.

Bay Fried Rice

Bay fried rice is a favourite at Indian weddings. The aroma of the bay leaves combined with the basmati rice is a great accompaniment to any curry dish.

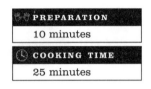

PREPARATION
10 minutes

COOKING TIME
25 minutes

INGREDIENTS

275g (10oz) basmati rice

50g (2oz) unsalted butter

1/2 tsp cumin seeds

3 bay leaves

2 black cardamoms

2 cloves

1 medium sized onion, finely chopped

1 tsp salt

1 tsp ginger pulp

1 tsp garlic pulp

500ml (20fl oz) water

METHOD

- Wash the rice and soak in cold water for 10-15 minutes.
- Melt the butter over a medium heat and stir-fry the cumin seeds for 2-3 minutes. Add the bay leaves, cardamoms, cloves and onion and continue to fry until the onion turns brown. Stir frequently. Add the salt, ginger and garlic.
- Drain the rice then add it to the pan and stir-fry for 1 minute.
- Add the water and bring to the boil. Cover the pan and simmer for 15 minutes without lifting the lid.
- Remove the pan from the heat and set aside undisturbed for around 10 minutes. Stir a fork through the rice before serving.

Chicken Biryani
(Murgh Biryani)

There are a few different methods of cooking this dish. Some people tend to cook the meat and rice together, although this is not absolutely necessary.

What we do is go down to the local supermarket and buy half a roast chicken, and break it up into fairly large chunks. This could be classed as cheating, but it certainly saves time and does the job.

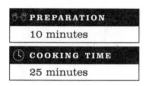

PREPARATION
10 minutes

COOKING TIME
25 minutes

INGREDIENTS

750ml (24fl oz) water

175g (6oz) basmati rice

2 black cardamoms, bruised

6 cloves

60ml (2fl oz) oil

1 small onion halved, and cut to form thin crescent shaped slices

1 tbsp garlic pulp

2 tsp garam masala

1 tsp red chilli powder

1 tsp ground cumin

1 tsp fenugreek leaves

1 tsp salt

500g (1lb) cooked chicken

50g (2oz) garden peas

50g (2oz) blanched almonds

$1/4$ tsp orange food colouring

To garnish:

1 hard-boiled egg, sliced

1 tomato, chopped

A sprinkle of cress

METHOD

• Wash the rice in warm water at least 3-4 times and drain. Pour the water in a saucepan and bring to the boil.

• Add the rice, black cardamoms and cloves and cook for around 15 minutes, drain and set aside.

• Meanwhile, heat the oil in a large saucepan and fry the onion until light brown. Add the garlic, garam masala, red chilli powder, ground cumin, fenugreek leaves and salt and stir-fry for 2 minutes.

• Add the chicken and stir well for a further 2 minutes. Add the garden peas and blanched almonds, bring to a simmer and carefully add in the rice, stirring continuously.

• Once the two are combined, add the orange food colouring.

• If the rice is too moist, boil rapidly, stirring to prevent it from sticking to the saucepan. Place the biryani on a serving dish and garnish with the chopped tomatoes, sliced eggs, and cress.

16. DRINKS

Lassi

Lassi is becoming popular throughout the world. Made from a combination of yoghurt and milk, it is normally consumed in hot countries to replace the loss of body fluids.

There are many types of lassi (pronounced Lussee), this version is called sweet (meeta) lassi. This is very easy to make and ideal for outdoor summer food parties especially for those who find that the spicy food has been too much for them.

PREPARATION
5 minutes

INGREDIENTS

300 ml (10fl oz) plain natural yoghurt

300 ml (10fl oz) chilled milk

Juice of half a lemon

2 tsp white sugar

a few ice cubes

METHOD

Put the yoghurt, milk, juice from the lemon, and sugar into a liquidiser and blend for about 1 minute. Pour the lassi into glasses and serve, topped with ice cubes.

Indian Tea

This delicately spiced tea is very popular in colder parts of the world.

PREPARATION
10-15 minutes

INGREDIENTS

300ml (10fl oz) milk

300ml (10fl oz) water

4 cloves

4 green cardamoms

2 cinnamon sticks 5cm (2-inches) long

2 tea bags

sugar to taste (optional)

METHOD

Put the milk and water into a saucepan and bring to the boil. Add the spices and simmer for 10 minutes. Add the teabags and slowly bring back to the boil. Brew for 3-5 minutes. Strain into a teapot and serve with or without sugar.

Mango Punch with Vodka

A lovely drink to welcome your guests with, and very simple to make. We've served this many a time, especially during the festive season.

PREPARATION

10 minutes

INGREDIENTS

3 ripe mangoes, peeled, stoned and chopped

2 tbsp of sugar

570ml (20fl oz/1 pint) water

175ml (6fl oz) vodka or more if you prefer

METHOD

Blend the chopped mangoes until they begin to look like pulp. Add the sugar and water and blend for a further minute. Add the vodka, mix in well with a spoon and serve chilled with ice cubes.

Nimbu Pani

Nimbu means lemon, this is the perfect refreshing drink for the hot weather or to accompany a spicy meal.

PREPARATION
5 minutes

INGREDIENTS

1 tsp salt

2 tbsp caster sugar

570ml (20fl oz/1pint) water

Juice of 1 lemon

Ice cubes

6 slices of lemon

METHOD

Put the salt and sugar in the water and stir until dissolved. Stir in the lemon juice. Put the ice cubes in glasses and strain the nimbu pani into the glasses. Top with the sliced lemon.

Grape Sherbet

This is good after a meal or for breakfast. Keep chilled.

PREPARATION

5 minutes

INGREDIENTS

200g (7oz) white seedless grapes

1 litre (40fl oz) water

50g (caster sugar)

1 tbsp lemon juice

$^1/_4$ tsp salt

Some ice cubes

METHOD

In a large bowl crush the grapes with a potato masher. Add the water and strain. Stir in the sugar until dissolved. Stir in the lemon juice and salt and serve with ice.

17. THE BASIC SAUCE

This can be made in a large quantity and then frozen in batches. This sauce is for the regular home cook and it lets you have a dish prepared in 20 or 30 minutes with the full authentic taste of an Indian meal.

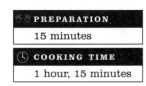

PREPARATION
15 minutes

COOKING TIME
1 hour, 15 minutes

INGREDIENTS

15 large onions, finely chopped (try and do this in a blender)

1 tsp salt

1/2 tsp cumin seeds

500 ml (20fl oz) warm water

6 tbsp of oil

1 tsp garam masala

2 tbsp ginger pulp

1 tbsp garlic pulp

1/2 tsp turmeric powder

1/2 tsp red chilli powder

2 tbsp coconut cream

4 tbsp of tomato paste

2 tomatoes quartered

2.5 cm (1-inch) cinnamon stick

4 cloves

2 bay leaves

4 green cardamoms

METHOD

- Put the onions into a pot along with the salt and cumin seeds.
- Add the warm water and bring to the boil, covering the pot with the lid and lower the heat to a medium setting. Stir occasionally.
- After around 40 minutes remove the lid and add the oil, garam masala, ginger pulp, garlic pulp, turmeric powder, chilli powder, coconut cream, tomato paste, tomatoes, cinnamon stick, cloves and bay leaves. Stir in well and cook for another 20 minutes with the lid off, this time stirring every 5 minutes.
- Remove the cinnamon stick and bay leaves. Use a blender to reduce the mixture to a pulp and continue to cook for a further 30 minutes on a low heat.
- This sauce is now ready for immediate use with a variety of accompaniments, some suggestions would be to pour over hot chips, fried chicken, kebabs or just to basically enhance your meal.

CELEBRITIES' FAVOURITE CURRY AND SPICE RECIPES

Ex-Scotland Rugby Internationalist and British Lion, John describes this as one of his favourite dishes. Although it's not strictly Indian (it's from Malaysia), it does have that spice 'value' that any Indian chef would be delighted with.

John Beattie's Nasi Goreng

I grew up as a kid in Borneo and Malaysia, and this easily prepared dish could be bought from road-side stalls. 'Nasi' means rice and 'Goreng' means fried, and the quantities of each item aren't important as you never make the dish the same way twice.

It hardly takes 15 minutes for a piping hot, spicy piece of heaven, but don't try to cook quantities that are too large.

Serve with an ice cold beer straight from the bottle on a sunny Friday evening and contemplate taking a month off work. I promise, it's paradise.

INGREDIENTS

PREPARATION
15 minutes

COOKING TIME
15 minutes

1 cup rice

1 medium sized onion

2 rashers of bacon

1 clove of garlic

2 small mushrooms

Nutmeg oil

1 half cup of peas

1 chicken breast

6 large tiger prawns

1 egg

Curry Powder

2.5cm (1-inch) cube of root ginger

Soy sauce

Sweet chilli sauce

2 sprigs of coriander or lemon grass

Salt and pepper to taste

METHOD

- Wash and rinse a cupful or maybe a spot more of rice a couple of times in a large pot, then add plenty of boiling water to cover and boil for around 8 minutes until ready.
- Sieve the rice and leave it to drain then fluff it up to dry it off. (If you have rice left over from a previous meal, use this as it's better.)
- Cut up an onion, a couple of rashers of bacon and a garlic clove, 1 or 2 small mushrooms, put them in some oil (preferably nutmeg) in a large hot frying pan or wok, and fry them until the onions are brown.
- Meanwhile, put a handful of peas on to simmer in another pot.
- Add a chopped-up chicken breast to the frying onions, and a pinch of curry powder or curry paste, a hint of ginger, plus a spot of soy sauce and some salt. Fry, stirring all the time. When the chicken is just about cooked add 6 or 7 large peeled tiger prawns and continue to stir until the prawns are pink and cooked through.
- Add the boiled rice and stir, turning and frying the rice until it's piping hot and cooked a little more.
- Add some more soy sauce, just a little, to colour it, and sprinkle on some salt and pepper. Make a hole in the middle of the rice mixture, exposing the frying pan in the middle. Crack an egg into this, keep stirring the egg in the well in the middle of the rice until it's cooked, then fold it into the rice. Don't fold it in before it's cooked.
- Add some sweet chilli sauce to the Nasi Goreng for a tang. Drain the peas and add them too, garnish the dish with some coriander leaves or lemon grass.

One of the best known faces on television in Scotland and everyone's favourite newsreader, Jackie is the anchor for BBC Scotland's **Reporting Scotland** evening news, as well as the presenter of BBC Scotland Hogmanay programmes.

Jackie is very enthusiastic about healthy eating and exercises regularly so her offering is clearly a healthy option.

Jackie Bird's Curried Chicken Salad with Avocado Dressing

PREPARATION
10 minutes plus 1 hour refrigeration

COOKING TIME
20 minutes

INGREDIENTS

500g (1lb) Chicken breast fillets

$1/2$ tsp salt

$1/4$ tsp ground turmeric

1 tsp curry powder

3 tbsp of oil

2 celery sticks, chopped

$1/2$ cucumber, sliced

4 green shallots, chopped

1 sprig of fresh parsley, chopped

Avocado Dressing:

$1/2$ tsp garlic pulp

60 ml (2fl oz) water

60 ml (2fl oz) French dressing

1 firm avocado sliced thinly.

METHOD

- With a sharp knife slit the chicken fillets in 2-3 places. Rub the chicken with the salt, ground turmeric and curry powder.
- Heat the oil over a medium heat in a large frying pan. Add the chicken fillets and cook for 15 minutes, or until tender, turning regularly.
- Remove from the pan, and set aside.
- Combine the celery, cucumbers, shallots and parsley in a bowl and mix well.
- Slice the chicken fillets and mix into the salad.
- Cover and refrigerate for 1 hour before serving.
- For the avocado dressing, blend all the ingredients until smooth. When the salad is ready to serve, cover it with the dressing.

The former Scotland football team manager and SFA Technical Director of Football is now manager of Preston North End. Craig, who comes from Ayrshire, was a regular customer in many local Ayrshire curry houses and he will be maintaining his curry habits down south.

Craig Brown's Chicken Tikka Masala

PREPARATION

15 minutes plus marinading overnight for the tikka

COOKING TIME

20 minutes plus 15 minutes to cook the tikka

INGREDIENTS

500g (1lb) Chicken tikka

(See recipe for chicken tikka kebab on p55)

4 tbsp of oil

1 medium sized onion, chopped

1 tsp garlic pulp

1 tsp ginger pulp

1 tbsp tomato paste

$\frac{1}{2}$ tsp ground turmeric

$\frac{1}{2}$ tsp ground cumin

$\frac{1}{2}$ tsp ground coriander

$\frac{1}{2}$ tsp garam masala

$\frac{1}{2}$ tsp red chilli powder

12ml (4fl oz) warm water

1 tsp salt

250ml (8fl oz) single cream

2 tbsp of ground almonds

METHOD

• Heat the oil over a medium heat in a saucepan, and gently fry the onion until light brown. Add the ginger, garlic and tomato paste and stir-fry for around 1 minute.

• Stir in the ground turmeric, ground cumin, ground coriander, garam masala and the red chilli powder and cook for around 1 minute.

• Gently stir in the warm water, add the salt and cook for 3-4 minutes.

• Stir in the single cream, add the chicken, turn the heat to low, cover the saucepan with a lid and cook for 5 minutes.

• Remove the lid from the saucepan and stir in the ground almonds.

• Cover the saucepan with a lid and simmer for 10 minutes and serve with rice or bread of your choice.

Phil Cunningham and Aly Bain are Scotland's most famous folk duo. Phil was approached in a pub near the BBC in Glasgow and asked to supply a recipe. Here's what they've given us.

Phil Cunningham and Aly Bain's Chicken Curry

This is a beautiful, simple, rich and fragrant dish, which we often cook on days off whilst touring. It is a great dish for people who don't like 'curry' curries! We have used this dish for Christmas dinner on more than one occasion.

As a lower fat alternative, use fat free yoghurt and NO CREAM!! Mix 1 tsp of dijon mustard for every 200 ml of yoghurt to stabilise and prevent from separating.

Also, if you have no saffron, use a level tsp of ground turmeric instead. Add this to the onions at the same time as the cardamom powder.

PREPARATION
15 minutes

COOKING TIME
30 minutes

INGREDIENTS

Oil or ghee to fry onions and chicken

3 medium sized onions, finely chopped

20 green cardamom pods

1kg (2lbs) boned skinless chicken cut into 2.5cm (1-inch) cubes

1 tbsp finely chopped garlic

1 tbsp finely chopped root ginger

1 tsp Indian chilli powder (Degi Mirch)

$\frac{1}{2}$ tsp black cumin seeds (ground)

1 tsp white cumin seeds (ground)

12 black peppercorns (ground)

(We use an electric coffee grinder which we have exclusively for grinding spices. Great device!)

8 fl oz yoghurt

4 fl oz single cream

good pinch of saffron

salt to taste

METHOD

- In a good heavy pan, fry the onions over a medium to high heat until golden brown. Well browned onions are essential for a good gravy!
- Remove the onions with a slotted spoon and set aside.
- Grind the cardamoms into a fine powder and mix with the reserved onions. Leave to infuse.
- Fry the chicken pieces a few at a time in the remaining oil (over a medium heat) until white all over.
- Add the garlic and ginger, stir and fry for 2 minutes.
- Add the chilli, ground black and white cumin, stir well and fry for a further 2 minutes.
- Add the ground peppercorns, stir and fry for a further minute.
- Mix together the yoghurt and cream, and add this to the meat gradually, stirring constantly. Add salt to taste. Cover and simmer until tender.
- Once tender, add the onion and cardamom, stir and simmer further to marry the flavours.
- Gently roast the saffron in a dry frying pan, this only takes seconds so be careful not to burn it! Crumble this into the pot for the last 2 minutes of cooking.
- Serve with boiled rice.

After a varied apprenticeship in journalism and local radio broadcasting, John Inverdale was one of the first sports reporters on Radio 5 Live and covered many major sporting events including the Olympic Games, the Rugby world cup, Wimbledon, and the Ryder Cup.

He was named Sony Broadcaster of the Year in 1997 for the network's drivetime show **John Inverdale Nationwide**. The move to television broadcasting brought five series of BBC One's acclaimed sports chat show **On Side** and the investigative sports series **On The Line**. Other BBC credits include **Rugby Special** as well as **Grandstand**, **Sunday Grandstand** and **The World's Strongest Man**. John's biggest sporting passion is rugby union and he is closely involved with Esher RFC. He is also a self-confessed pop trivia bore!

John Inverdale's Naan Bread (Leavened Bread)

The traditional way to cook naan bread is in a clay oven, but don't worry, as it can taste just as good when baked in an ordinary domestic conventional oven. (If you're lucky enough to own an Aga, the results are great!).

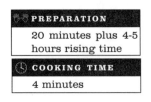

PREPARATION
20 minutes plus 4-5 hours rising time

COOKING TIME
4 minutes

INGREDIENTS

500g (1lb) plain white flour, plus extra for dusting

1 tsp baking powder

$\frac{1}{2}$ tsp salt

2 tbsp plain, unsweetened yoghurt

120ml (4fl oz) pasteurised milk

1 tsp sugar

$\frac{1}{2}$ tsp baker's yeast

50g (2oz) melted butter

METHOD

- Sift the flour in a large bowl together with the baking powder and salt.
- Mix in the yoghurt, milk, sugar and yeast. Add a little extra water or milk if necessary – this is to ensure the dough has a hard consistency. Knead well for at least 10 minutes.
- Cover with a damp tea towel and set aside allowing the dough to rise for 4-5 hours.
- Divide the dough into 14-16 balls. Hold each ball between your palms and rotate in a circular motion until it is smooth and round, flatten the ball into a round cake and, using a combination of rolling and pulling, form into elongated shapes.
- Lay each naan out on a baking tray, and brush with the melted butter.
- Bake in a pre-heated oven for 4 minutes on both sides until toasted blisters appear.
- Serve with your main curry dish.

A firm favourite with sports fans across the UK, Hazel is one of the most versatile presenters in sports broadcasting and her work has taken her across the world to the Olympics and Commonwealth games. Despite her schedule, Hazel managed to spare some time to give us her favourite spicy dish.

Hazel Irvine's Lemon Chicken with French Beans

PREPARATION
15 minutes

COOKING TIME
40-45 minutes

INGREDIENTS

4 tbsp of oil

2 medium sized onions, finely chopped

4 bay leaves

1/4 tsp onion seeds

1 tsp ginger pulp

1 tsp garlic pulp

1 tsp red chilli powder

1 tsp dried mango powder

1 tsp salt

1/2 tsp garam masala

3 tbsp lemon juice

500g (1lb) boneless, skinless chicken cut into 2.5cm (1-inch) cubes

450ml (15fl oz) warm water

250g (8oz) frozen french beans

2 sprigs of fresh coriander, finely chopped

Lemon wedges for decoration

METHOD

- Heat the oil over a medium heat in a large saucepan, and fry the onions, bay leaves and onion seeds until the onions turn light brown.
- Reduce the heat to low, add the ginger, garlic, red chilli powder, mango powder, salt, garam masala and lemon juice and stir-fry for around 5 minutes.
- Add the chicken and stir-fry for another 3-4 minutes. Increase the heat to medium, gradually add the water and French beans, cover the saucepan with a lid and simmer for 25 minutes, checking and stirring occasionally.
- Stir in the freshly chopped coriander, transfer to a serving dish, decorate with the lemon wedges and serve with bread or rice of your choice.

The 'White Shark' of Scottish rugby was a member of the famous 1990 Grand Slam team and was renowned as a great touring player with the British Lions. As a Border farmer, it's not surprising that John has chosen a firey, beef-based dish for the book. Is this the secret of his rugby success?

John Jeffrey's Beef with Carrots and Jalapeno peppers

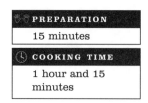

PREPARATION

15 minutes

COOKING TIME

1 hour and 15 minutes

INGREDIENTS

500g (1lb) beef, cut into 2.5cm (1-inch) cubes

1 tsp ginger pulp

1 tbsp garlic pulp

1 tsp salt

4 tbsp of cooking oil

1 medium sized onion, chopped

1 tsp ground turmeric

1 black cardamom

1 tsp ground black pepper

1/2 tsp fenugreek leaves

1 tbsp tomato paste

1 tomato, chopped

1 carrot peeled and chopped

3 fresh jalapeno peppers, chopped

300ml (10fl oz) warm water

1/2 tsp garam masala

2 sprigs of fresh coriander, finely chopped

METHOD

• Place the cubed beef in a large bowl, rub the ginger, garlic and salt into the lamb, cover and set aside.

• Heat the oil over a medium heat in a large saucepan and fry the onions gently until light brown.

• Add the marinaded beef and fry until it changes colour. Add the ground turmeric, black cardamom, black pepper, fenugreek leaves, tomato paste and chopped tomato and continue to fry for 5 minutes stirring frequently.

• Lower the heat and add the carrots and jalapeno peppers and fry for 2 minutes, stirring the saucepan once.

• Add the warm water, and cover the saucepan with a lid (leaving a gap of half an inch) and simmer for about 50 minutes, checking and stirring occasionally.

• Stir in the garam masala and fresh coriander and serve with bay fried rice or bread of your choice.

Lady Claire Macdonald's Cold Spicy Lemon and Orange Chicken

©Iain Smith, Skye Photo Centre.

In June 2002, Neil Wilson, the publisher of this book, held a party in his garden. He served Cold Spicy Lemon and Orange Chicken from Lady Claire Macdonald's **Simply Seasonal** cookbook and I thought it was simply delicious ... 'Neil,' I said, 'any chance of getting this in our book?'

PREPARATION
15 minutes

COOKING TIME
15 minutes

This dish looks so attractive when it is ready to serve that there's no need to worry about any garnish. It's all in the ingredients!

INGREDIENTS

(Serves 4)

5 fl oz/150ml natural yoghurt

1½ tbsp orange juice

1½ tbsp lemon juice

About 2.5cm (1-inch) fresh ginger, peeled and chopped

1 tsp dried chilli flakes

1 tsp coriander seeds, pulverised in a mortar with a pestle

½ tsp ground turmeric

Sea salt

7 fl oz/200 ml full-fat crème fraiche

About 2 tbsp oil, either sunflower or olive

1 bay leaf

2 tsp 4-colour mixed peppercorns, crushed

3 cardamom pods, crushed

1-1½ lb/450-700g chicken breast meat, cut into 2.5cm (1-inch) cubes

1 tbsp chopped coriander leaves

About 12 cherry tomatoes, halved

METHOD

• In a mixing bowl stir together the yoghurt, orange and lemon juice, the ginger, dried chillies, coriander, turmeric, salt and crème fraîche.

• In a sauté pan heat the oil with the bay leaf, the peppercorns and the cardamom, and cook together over a moderate heat for a couple of minutes.

• Then pour in the yoghurt and crème fraîche mixture and cook for a further minute.

• Add the cut-up chicken and cook, stirring from time to time, for 5-8 minutes.

• Stir in the chopped coriander leaves and halved tomatoes, then cook for a further few minutes until the tomatoes have heated through. Leave it to cool.

• Serve cold with boiled basmati rice or bread.

The voice of football on BBC TV Scotland and Reporting Scotland, Rob is a very keen footballer himself (and a Ross County fan to boot).

Rob Maclean's Goan Lamb or Beef Curry

PREPARATION
20 minutes

COOKING TIME
1 hour

INGREDIENTS

4 tbsp of oil

1 medium sized onion, chopped

500g (1lb) lamb or beef cut into cubes

2 tbsp garlic pulp

1 tsp ginger pulp

1 tsp ground turmeric powder

4 green chillies seeded, and finely chopped

50g (2oz) creamed coconut

1 tsp salt

2 sprigs of fresh coriander, finely chopped

1 tsp tomato paste

1 tsp aniseed powder

250ml (8fl oz) warm water

METHOD

- Heat the oil in a large saucepan on a medium heat, and fry the onion until light brown.
- Add the meat, garlic, ginger, turmeric powder and the chopped chillies, mix well and fry, stirring occasionally, for 10 minutes until the meat is dry.
- Stir in the creamed coconut and fry for 2-3 minutes. Add the salt, freshly chopped coriander, tomato paste, aniseed powder and stir in the warm water.
- Cover and gently cook for 50 minutes, checking and stirring occasionally or until the meat is tender.
- Serve with rice or bread of your choice.

Now the voice of the **PM** evening programme on BBC Radio 4, Eddie worked at BBC Scotland alongside me (Ali) in the newsroom in the late 80s and 90s. He is a serious foodie, and is always up for a curry as his delicious contribution confirms.

Eddie Mair's
Lamb with Butterbeans

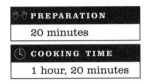

PREPARATION

20 minutes

COOKING TIME

1 hour, 20 minutes

INGREDIENTS

1kg (2.2lbs) leg or shoulder of lamb

6 tablespoons of cooking oil

2 medium sized onions, finely chopped

1 tbsp garlic pulp

2 tsp ginger pulp

1 tsp red chilli powder

1 tsp ground turmeric

1 tsp cumin seeds

2 black cardamoms

6 cloves

2 tbsp tomato paste

1 tsp salt

1 tomato quartered

600ml (20fl oz) warm water

150g (6oz) butter beans, soaked overnight in plenty of cold water

1 tsp garam masala

1 tbsp lemon juice

2 sprigs of fresh coriander leaves, finely chopped

METHOD

• Trim off any fat from the lamb and cut into 2.5cm (1-inch) cubes.

• Heat the oil over a medium heat and fry the onions until soft. Add the ginger and garlic and stir-fry for around 1-2 minutes.

• Add the red chilli powder, ground turmeric, cumin seeds, black cardamoms, cloves, tomato paste and salt, adjust the heat to low and fry for around 3-4 minutes.

• Add the meat and quartered tomato, turn the heat up to medium and fry for 5 minutes stirring frequently.

• Add the warm water and bring to the boil, cover and simmer for around 50 minutes (checking and stirring occasionally). Drain, and add the butterbeans to the pot, cover and cook for a further 15-20 minutes or until the meat is tender.

• Add the lemon juice, stir in the freshly chopped coriander and serve with rice or bread of your choice.

maggie's centre
cancer caring centre

The first Maggie's Cancer Caring Centre opened in 1996, in a converted stable block in the grounds of the Western General Hospital. It was conceived by a remarkable woman, Maggie Keswick Jencks, when she herself was treated for breast cancer. Maggie recognised the difficulties of accessing information and on-going support which help people cope with the issues cancer brings up.

To meet these needs Maggie's Centres have developed a unique support programme which has proved highly effective for people with cancer, family members, friends and their medical consultants. Health professionals from hospitals across the UK came to visit Maggie's Edinburgh and as a result centres are being developed across Scotland in Glasgow, Dundee, Fife, Highlands and then the rest of the UK.

All Maggie's services are free and no appointment is necessary to visit. For more details call 0131 537 3131.

INDEX OF RECIPES AND INGREDIENTS